LETTERS
TO ALICE

FAY WELDON

LETTERS TO ALICE

ON FIRST READING
JANE AUSTEN

A Harvest/HBJ Book

HARCOURT BRACE JOVANOVICH, PUBLISHERS

San Diego   New York   London

Published by arrangement with Taplinger Publishing Co., Inc.
First published in the U.K. by Michael Joseph Ltd. and The Rainbird
Publishing Group Ltd. 1984

LIBRARY OF CONGRESS CATALOGING-IN-PUBLICATION DATA
Weldon, Fay.
    Letters to Alice on first reading Jane Austen.
    "A Harvest/HBJ book."
    1. Austen, Jane, 1775-1817—Criticism and
interpretation. 2. Fiction. 3. Books and reading.
[PR4037.W45] 1986   823'.7   86-221
ISBN 0-15-650981-4 (pbk.)

Printed in the United States of America
First Harvest/HBJ edition 1986

ABCDEFGHIJ

Contents

To my mother (who is not, I may say, the one in this book, this epistolary novel; *she* is an entirely invented character, along with Alice, Enid and so forth) to whom I owe such morality and wisdom as I have.

The City of Invention

Cairns, Australia, October

My dear Alice,

It was good to get your letter. I am a long way from home here; almost in exile. And you ask me for advice, which is warming, and makes me believe I must know something; or at any rate more than you. The impression of knowing less and less, the older one gets, is daunting. The last time I saw you, you were two, blonde and cherubic. Now, I gather, you are eighteen, you dye your hair black and green with vegetable dye, and your mother, my sister, is perturbed. Perhaps your writing to me is a step towards your and her eventual reconciliation? I shall not interfere between the two of you: I shall confine myself to the matters you raise.

Namely, Jane Austen and her books. You tell me, in passing, that you are doing a college course in English Literature, and are obliged to read Jane Austen; that you find her boring, petty and irrelevant and, that as the world is in crisis, and the future catastrophic, you cannot imagine what purpose there can be in your reading her.

My dear child! My dear pretty little Alice, now with black and green hair.

How can I hope to explain Literature to you, with its capital 'L'? You are bright enough. You could read when you were four. But then, sensibly, you turned to television for your window on the world: you slaked your appetite for information, for stories, for beginnings, middles and ends, with the easy tasty substances of the screen in the living room, and (if I remember your mother rightly) no doubt in your bedroom too. You lulled yourself to sleep with visions of violence, and the cruder strokes of human action and reaction; stories in which every simple action has a simple motive, nothing is inexplicable, and even God moves in an un-mysterious way. And now you realize this is not enough: you have an inkling there is something more, that your own feelings and responses are a thousand times more complex than this tinny televisual representation of reality has ever suggested: you have, I suspect and hope, intimations of infinity, of the romance of creation, of the wonder of love, of the glory of existence; you look around for companions in your wild new comprehension, your sudden vision, and you see the same zonked-out stares, the same pale faces and dyed cotton-wool hair, and you turn, at last, to education, to literature, and books – and find them closed to you.

Do not despair, little Alice. Only persist, and thou shalt see, Jane Austen's all in all to thee. A coconut fell from a tree just now, narrowly missing the head of a fellow guest, here at this hotel at the edge of a bright blue tropical sea, where sea-stingers in the mating season (which cannot be clearly defined) and at paddling depth, grow invisible tentacles forty feet long, the merest touch of which will kill a child; and any easily shockable adult too, no doubt. Stay out of the sea, and the coconuts get you!

But there is a copy of Jane Austen's *Emma* here, in the small bookshelf, and it's well-thumbed. The other books are yet more tattered; they are thrillers and romances, temporary things. These books open a little square window on the world and set the puppets parading outside for you to observe. They bear little resemblance to human beings, to anyone you ever met or are likely to meet. These characters exist for purposes of plot, and the books they appear in do not threaten the reader in any way; they do not suggest that he or she should reflect, let alone *change*. But then, of course, being so safe, they defeat themselves, they can never enlighten. And because they don't enlighten, they are unimportant. (Unless, of course, they are believed, when they become dangerous. To *believe* a Mills & Boon novel reflects real life, is to live in perpetual disappointment. You are meant to believe while the reading lasts, and not a moment longer.) These books, the tattered ones, the thrillers and romances, are interchangeable. They get used to light the barbecues, when the sun goes down over the wild hills, and there's a hunger in the air – not just for steak and chilli sauce, but a real human demand for living, sex, experience, change. The pages flare up, turn red, turn black, finish. The steak crackles, thanks to a copy of *Gorki Park*. Everyone eats. Imperial Caesar, dead and turned to clay, would stop a hole to keep the wind away!

But no one burns *Emma*. No one would dare. There is too much concentrated here: too much history, too much respect, too much of the very essence of civilization, which is, I must tell you, connected to its Literature. It's Literature, with a capital 'L', as opposed to just books. Hitler, of course, managed to burn Literature as well as Just Books at the Reichstag fire, and his nation's cultural past with it, and no one has ever forgiven or forgotten. You have to be really *bad* to burn Literature.

How can I explain this phenomenon to you? How can I convince you of the pleasures of a good book, when you have McDonald's around one corner and *An American Werewolf in London* around the next? I suffer myself from the common nervous dread of literature. When I go on holiday, I read first the thrillers, then the sci-fi, then the instructional books, then *War and Peace*, or whatever book it is I know I ought to read, ought to have read, half want to read and only when reading want to fully. Of course one dreads it: of course it is overwhelming: one both anticipates and fears the kind of swooning, almost erotic pleasure that a good passage in a good book gives; as something nameless *happens*. I don't know what it is that happens: is it the pleasure of mind meeting mind, untramelled by flesh? Of the inchoation of our own experience suddenly given shape and form? Why yes, we cry: yes, yes, that is how it is! But we have to be strong to want to know: if something, suddenly, is going to *happen* as we encounter the *Idea*, and discover it adds up to more than the parts which comprise it: understand that *Idea* is more than the sum of experience. It takes courage, to comprehend not just what we are, but why we are.

Perhaps they will explain it to you better, at your English Literature course. I hope so. I rather doubt it. In such places (or so it seems to me), those in charge are taking something they cannot quite understand but have an intimation is remarkable, and breaking it down into its component parts in an attempt to discover its true nature. As well take a fly to bits, and hope that the bits will explain the creature. You will know more, but understand less. You will have more information, and less wisdom. I do not wish (much) to insult Departments of English Literature, nor to suggest for one moment that you would do better out of their care than in it: I am just saying be careful. And I speak as one studied by Literature

Departments (a few) and in Women's Studies Courses (more) and I say 'one' advisedly, because it is not just my novels (legitimate prey, as works of what they care to call the creative imagination) but *me* they end up wanting to investigate, and it is not a profitable study.

Now, as a writer of novels I am one thing: what you *read* of mine has gone to third or fourth draft: it is fiction: that is to say, it is a properly formulated vision of the world. But myself living, talking, giving advice, writing this letter, is only, please remember, in first draft. As someone trying to persuade you to read and enjoy *Emma*, and *Persuasion*, and *Mansfield Park*, and *Northanger Abbey*, and *Pride and Prejudice*, and (on occasion) *Sense and Sensibility*, and (quite often) *Lady Susan*, I am quite another. Believe me or disbelieve me, as you choose. But hear me out.

You must *read*, Alice, before it's too late. You must fill your mind with the invented images of the past: the more the better. Literary images of Beowulf, and The Wife of Bath, and Falstaff and Sweet Amaryllis in the Shade, and Elizabeth Bennet, and the Girl in the Green Hat – and Rabbit Hazel of *Watership Down*, if you must. These images, apart from anything else, will help you put the two and twos of life together, and the more images your mind retains, the more wonderful will be the star-studded canopy of experience beneath which you, poor primitive creature that you are, will shelter: the nearer you will creep to the great blazing beacon of the Idea which animates us all.

No? Too rich and embarrassing an image? Would you prefer me to say, more safely, 'Literature stands at the gates of civilization, holding back greed, rage, murder, and savagery of all kinds?' I am not too happy with this myself: I think I am as likely, these days, to be raped and murdered in my bed within the gates of civilization as without. Unless civilization itself is failing, because literature has stepped aside and we now merely stare at images? Unless we watch television, and do not read, and so are losing the power of reflection? In which case it is only Departments of English Literature which stand between us and our doom!

No? I see I am trying to define literature by what it does, not by what it is. By experience, not Idea.

Let's try another way. Let me put to you another notion.

Try this. Frame it in your mind as a TV cameraman frames a shot, getting Sue Ellen nicely centred. Let me give you, let me share with you, the City of Invention. For what novelists do (I have decided, for the purposes of your conversion) is to build Houses of the Imagination, and where houses cluster together there is a city. And what a city this one is, Alice! It is the nearest we poor mortals can get to the Celestial City: it glitters and glances with life, and gossip, and colour, and fantasy: it is brilliant, it is illuminated, by day by the sun of enthusiasm and by night by the moon of inspiration. It has its towers and pinnacles, its commanding heights and its swooning depths: it has public buildings and worthy ancient monuments, which some find boring and others magnificent. It has its central districts and its suburbs, some salubrious, some seedy, some safe, some frightening. Those who founded it, who built it, house by house, are the novelists, the writers, the poets. And it is to this city that the readers come, to admire, to learn, to marvel and explore.

Let us look round the city: become acquainted with it, make it our eternal, our immortal home. Looming over everything, of course, heart of the City, is the great Castle Shakespeare. You see it whichever way you look. It rears its head into the clouds, reaching into the celestial sky, dominating everything around. It's a rather uneven building, frankly. Some complain it's shoddy, and carelessly constructed in parts, others grumble that Shakespeare never built it anyway, and a few say the whole thing ought to be pulled down to make way for the newer and more relevant, and this prime building site released for younger talent: but the Castle keeps standing through the centuries and, build as others may they can never quite achieve the same grandeur; and the visitors keep flocking, and the guides keep training and re-training, finding yet new ways of explaining the old building. It's more than a life's work.

Here in this City of Invention, the readers come and go, by general invitation, sauntering down its leafy avenues, scurrying through its horrider slums, waving to each other across the centuries, up and down the arches of the years. When I say 'the arches of the years' it may well sound strange to you. But I know what I'm doing: it is you who are at fault. This is a phrase used by Francis

Thompson – a Catholic poet, late-nineteenth century – in his slightly ridiculous but haunting poem 'The Hound of Heaven':

> I fled Him, down the nights and down the days;
> I fled Him, down the arches of the years;

The poem is about God pursuing an escaping soul, lurching after him, hound-like. He gets him in the end, as a Mountie gets his man. (Another dusty image, no doubt; and one scarcely worth the taking out and dusting down.) When I refer to 'the arches of the years' I hope to convey the whole feeling-tone (as Freudians say of dreams) of the poem, both the power and the slight absurdity; *all* the poem in fact, in the five words of his that I choose, for the benefit of my sentence. Call it plagiarism, call it fellowship between writers, or resonance (since you're in a Dept. of Eng. Lit.). I don't suppose it matters much. It is the kind of thing writers used to depend upon in their attempts to get taken seriously, and now no longer can. We talk to an audience (and I say talk advisedly, rather than write: for contemporary authors are left largely with the writing down on paper of what they could as well speak, if only their listeners would stand still for long enough) and a generation which has read so little it understands only the vernacular. I don't think this matters much. I think that writers have to change and adapt. It is no use lamenting a past: people *now* are as valuable as people *then*. You will just have to take my word for it, that the words a writer uses, even now, go back and back into a written history. Words are not simple things: they take unto themselves, as they have through time, power and meaning: they did so then, they do so now.

I bet £500 you have not read 'The Hound of Heaven'.

But back to our City of Invention. Let me put it like this – writers create Houses of the Imagination, from whose doors the generations greet each other. You will always hear a great deal of enlivening dissension and discussion. Should Madame Bovary have munched the arsenic? Would Anna Karenina have gone under the train had Tolstoy been a woman, would Darcy have married Elizabeth anywhere else but in the City of Invention, and so on and so forth, in and out of the centuries.

And thus, by such discussion and such shared experience, do we understand ourselves and one another, and our pasts and our futures. It is in the literature, the novels, the fantasy, the fiction of the past, that you find *real* history, and not in text books. Thomas More's *Utopia* tells us as much about his own century, his own world, as the one he invented for the delectation of his peers.

Writers are privileged visitors here. They have a house or two of their own in the City, after all. Perhaps even well-thought of, and nicely maintained: or perhaps never much reckoned and falling into disrepair. But to have a house of any kind, even to have brought it only to planning stage, and have given up in despair, is to realize more fully the wonder of the City, and to know how its houses are built: to know also that though one brick may look much like another, and all builders go about their work in much the same way, some buildings will be good, some bad. And a very few, sometimes the least suspected, will last, and not crumble with the decades.

Writers, builders, good or bad, recognizing these things, are usually polite to one another, and a great deal kinder than the people who visit, as outsiders. Builders vary in intellect, aspiration, talent and efficiency; they build well or badly in different suburbs of the City. Some build because they need to, have to, live to, or believe they are appointed to, others to prove a point or to change the world. But to build at all requires courage, persistence, faith and a surplus of animation. A writer's *all*, Alice, is not taken up by the real world. There is something left over: enough for them to build these alternative, finite realities.

Jane Austen had a great deal left over. You could say that was because she didn't wear herself out physically running round the world, pleasing a husband or looking after children. (But that didn't save her from an early and unpleasant death.) And though this meant that she chose, perhaps, a safer, rather inward-looking site to build her houses (though what a pleasant, grassy, well-regarded mound it turned out to be), than she would otherwise have done, she gave herself, through her writing, another life that out-ran her own; a literary life. It was not, I am sure, what she set out to do. But it happened. She breathed in, as it were, into the source of her own energy, her own life, and breathed out a hundred different lives. She had energy enough to build. Some, of course – and I tend to be one of them – maintain that the constant energizing friction of wifehood, motherhood and domesticity, provides its own surging energy, and creates as powerful an inner life as does the prudent, contemplative, my-art-my-art-alone existence. Others deny it.

You get all kinds of writers, Alice. You get Dickens and St Theresa of Avila, you get wicked George Sand, surrounded by lovers and children, and you get Jane Austen. Writers deal with their lives as best they can, and their personalities, and the family and century into which they were born: they do what they must with their day-to-day existences, and build in the City of Invention.

It's getting crowded, these days, here as anywhere else. Look around. Almost nowhere that's not been built on! Unless they think of somewhere new, which they probably will: discover a new slope, or hillside, hitherto considered barren, which with a little ingenuity turns out to be fertile. The City as it is today, stretches far and wide, through dreary new suburbs to a misty horizon. All kinds of people choose to build here now, and not just those born to it. Non-vocational writers can put up a pretty fair representation of a proper house, and even get a number of enthusiastic visitors. The structure will crumble within the year, and then someone else will quickly use the site, fill the space on the Station Bookstall. But the result is that bus journeys into the centre of the city can seem to last for ever – so many books, just *so many*, on the way! – before you get to those wonderful places where the visitors flock and the tourists gasp with gratification, and that's where I want you to go, Alice. I know no one's ever set you a proper example. (Your mother reads books on tennis, I know: I doubt she's read a novel since an overdose of Georgette Heyer made her marry your father. Books can be dangerous.) I do not want you to be deprived of the pleasures of literature. You are, in spite of everything, my flesh and blood.

I can give you a physical location for the City. It lies at a mid-way point between the Road to Heaven and the Road to Hell; these two were depicted in the lithograph that used to hang on your mother's and my bedroom wall when we were children: before I took the broad and primrose Road to Hell, by going with our father when he left, and she stayed on the narrow, uphill path of righteousness that leads to Heaven, by remaining with our mother. What dramas there were then, little Alice, with your green and black hair! You have no idea how the world has changed in forty years.

Before you can properly appreciate Jane Austen, you do need to be, just a little, acquainted with the City: at any rate with its more important districts. Master builders work up on the heights, in the shadow of some great castle or other. They build whole streets, worthy and respectable. Mannstrasse, Melville Ave, Galsworthy Close. You need at least to know *where* they are. More fun, perhaps, to ferret out the places where an innocent has erected some glittering edifice almost by mistake – Tressell's *Ragged Trousered Philanthropists*, or Flora Thompson's *Lark Rise to Candleford* or James Stevens's *The Caretaker's Daughter* – or a child achieved what an adult can't. The path up to Daisy Ashford's *Young Visiters* is always thronged with delighted visitors. But it's pleasant going about anywhere, especially with company. You can wander up and down the more cosmopolitan areas, dip into Sartre, or Sagan, or through the humbler districts, saying: that's a good house for round here, or this one really lets the neighbourhood down! Sometimes you'll find quite a shoddy building so well placed and painted that it quite takes the visitor in, and the critics as well – and all cluster round, crying, 'Lo, a masterpiece!' and award it prizes. But the passage of time, the peeling of paint, the very lack of concerned visitors, reveals it in the end for what it is: a house of no interest or significance.

You will find that buildings rise and fall in the estimation of visitors, for no apparent reason. Who reads Arnold Bennett now, or Sinclair Lewis? But perhaps soon, with any luck, they'll be rediscovered. 'How interesting,' people will say, pushing open the creaking doors. 'How remarkable! Don't you feel the atmosphere here? So familiar, so true: the amazing masquerading as the ordinary? Why haven't we been here for so long?' And Bennett, Lewis, or whoever, will be rediscovered, and the houses of his imagination be renovated, restored, and hinges oiled so that doors open easily, and the builder, the writer, takes his rightful place again in the great alternative hierarchy.

Visitors, builders feel (even while asking them in and feeling insulted if they don't look around), are demanding and difficult people; the visitors seem to have no idea at all how tricky the building of Houses is. They think if only they had the time, they'd do it themselves. They say, such a life I've had! I really ought to put it all down some day; turn it into a book! And so indeed what a life they've had, but the mere recording of event does not make a book. Experience does not add up to Idea. It is easier for the reader to judge, by a thousand times, than for the writer to invent. The writer must summon his Idea out of nowhere, and his characters out of nothing, and catch words as they fly, and nail them to the page. The reader has something to go by and somewhere to start from, given to him freely and with great generosity by the writer. And still the reader feels free to find fault.

Some builders build their houses and refuse to open the door, so terrified of visitors are they. In drawers and cupboards all over the land, I'll swear, are the hidden manuscripts of perfectly publishable novels which, for lack of a brown envelope and a stamp and a little nerve, never see the light of day. Genius lasts, but I'm not so sure that it will necessarily *out*.

Sometimes when a builder opens the door of a newly finished house, and the crowds and critics rush in, he must wish he'd never opened the door. Hardy never wrote another novel after *Jude the Obscure* was published, so upsetting did the critics find it, and so upsetting did he find the critics.

Mind you, I see their point. *Jude the Obscure* stopped me reading for quite some time. I kept postponing my visits to the City for fear of what I might find there; the Giant Despair, for example, wandering the hitherto serene streets, zapping the unwary visitor on the head. Hardy, claimed the critics, was the one who had unlocked the cage and let the Giant loose: and then, worse, had opened the gates of the City and positively invited him in: had made it a dangerous place.

It's safer, you'll find, down among the Pre-Fabs, if it's safety you're after. Here the verges are neatly swept and Despair wears a muzzle, albeit the houses themselves lack all grandeur and aspiration. Surprising to see such flimsy structures built with such care and skill. Novels-from-films – film first, novel after – *Jaws*, *Alien*, *E.T.* – are so efficiently written as to all but pass for real creation, real invention, and not the calculated flights of reason that they are. There is no vision here, but an acute observation of what a mass audience wants to see and hear. Heart-strings twang, but don't vibrate. The windows in these Pre-Fabs have the blinds pulled down, and on the blinds are painted what you might reasonably see (reasonably for the City of Invention, that is) if they were raised – a beach scene, or a space ship, or an extra-terrestrial plodding about outside – but they are still only painted, albeit with wonderful conviction. And if you do raise the blinds, send them whirring up to the ceiling, where clean brisk straight edge meets clean brisk straight edge (nothing here of the softness of age, no mellow patina of the past) you will see out of the windows grey nothingness, and when the thrumming shark-fear music has died away, and the wistful songs of outer space, you may even hear the footfall of Despair outside and wonder just how fast his claws do grow, and if he gets even this far, and if he's snapped his muzzle free.

Quick, next door, to the rather solider hyped twin houses of *Scruples* and *Lace*. The blinds are frilly and expensive and very firmly pulled down. You're not supposed to look around too closely, once inside. You may not want to, much (and in any case, your comments aren't called for. You're supposed to pay your money at the door, and leave at once). These houses and others like them, are well enough made. They are calculated to divert and impress and often do – but do not take them seriously, Alice, and know them for what they are.

The good builders, the really good builders, carry a vision out of the real world and transpose it into the City of Invention, and refresh and enlighten the reader, so that on his, or her, return to reality, that reality itself is changed, however minutely. A book that has no base in an initial reality, written out of reason and not conviction, is a house built of – what shall we say? – bricks and no mortar? Walk into it, brush against a door frame, and the whole edifice falls down about your ears. Like the first little pig's house of straw, when the big bad wolf huffed and puffed.

Round the corner from the money-makers, the edges of the two suburbs running together, is the vast red-light district of Porno. Step into houses here at your peril: what you find inside is exciting enough, but the windows have no blinds at all, and there is real pain, torture, degradation and death out there. There are not even any curtains, just a nasty red flicker round the edges of the window frames, because this is where the city borders on Hell. Well, somewhere has to, just as someone has to be bottom of the class. But the suburb's grown too fast, it's unstoppable. Police forever roam the streets, to the mirth of the nudging, knowing, winking inhabitants, and occasionally manage to demolish a monstrosity, only to find a worse one springing up in its place. There's a good building or so, of course, round here, and visitors bus in from everywhere, sometimes on very respectable tours. They come in by the bus-load for *The Story of O* – it's so well constructed, they say: so elegantly made; look how graceful the lintels are, how delicately placed the beams – never mind where the whole thing's placed! And the French lady, Anais Nin, Henry Miller's friend, never built better than when she was down here, and well paid. You will find, if you insist, other light-fingered and enchanting structures up and down the streets, but they have the air of the witch's house in *Hansel and Gretel*. All smarties and gingerbread and delicious; but beware, the witch with her oven waits inside, and she's luring you in, to eat you up! Wait until you're older, Alice, and the pleasures of your own flesh desert you.

(You may not know, of course, who Henry Miller was. He was an American. He wrote *Tropic of Cancer* and *Tropic of Capricorn* back in the thirties, books explicitly sexual and much banned, and, with hindsight, exploitative of women. At the time he seemed the prophet of freedom, liberation, and imagination. His houses still stand.)

I used to spend a lot of time myself in the all-male suburb of Sci-Fi, in the days when it was formal and reliable and informed and only a few knew of its pleasures. Sci-Fi Town borders on the red-light district: the two areas blend easily, being all mind and no heart. The houses here are mostly new, though a few proud old structures still stand. Jules Verne and H. G. Wells were amongst the first to build. Aldous Huxley's *Brave New World* and George Orwell's *1984* are showpieces in that nowadays slightly shoddy main street, Utopia. (Utopia comes from the Greek, Alice, and means a Nowhere Place, not a Good Place, as many people think.) Thomas More's *Utopia* and Samuel Butler's *Erewhon* ('Nowhere' spelt backwards – well, more or less) were perhaps the finest and best buildings constructed here. But it's the same here as anywhere: districts become too quickly fashionable, groundspace over-priced, jerry-building is tempting: good buildings are torn down and replaced by inferior constructions and then the heart of the place is gone. No one writes about Utopias any more.

Science Fantasy, where these days the builders are for the most part women, is an area newly and brightly developed. But I for one still prefer to look out of windows and see futuristic nuts and bolts and the occasional bug-eyed monster rather than the strange shifting phantasms which you see up and down the new Fantasy Alley. (I am composing a reading list for you, incidentally. I shall send it under separate cover. An informed visitor to the City of Invention has a better time there than the naive and hopeful.)

Romance Alley is of course a charming place, as your mother, I am sure, will tell you. It's a boom town, too. The suburbs are increasingly popular for visitors who need time off from their own lives. (You don't need to know anything about the rest of the City to visit here. Enough to be naive and hopeful.) And it really is a pretty place. Everything is lavender-tinted, and the cottages have roses round the door, and knights ride by in shining armour, and amazingly beautiful young couples stroll by under the blossoming trees, though *he* perhaps has a slightly cruel mouth, and *she* a tendency to swoon.

Jane Austen is reputed to have fainted away when she came home from a walk with her sister, Cassandra, and was told by her mother, 'It's all settled. We're moving to Bath.' It was the first, they say, she'd heard of it. (Mind you, as I am fond of saying, they'll say anything!) She was twenty-five; she had lived all her life in the Vicarage at Steventon: her father, without notifying anyone, had decided to retire, and thought that Bath was as pleasant a place as any to go. None of us fainted the day my father came home and told my mother, my sister and myself that he was leaving us that day to live for ever with his sweetheart, whose existence he'd never hinted at before. What are we to make of that? That swooning has gone out of fashion? Or that a later female generation has become inured, by reason of a literature increasingly related to the realities of life, to male surprises? Jane Austen's books are studded with fathers indifferent to their families' (in particular their daughters') welfare, male whims taking priority, then as now, over female happiness. She observes it: she does not condemn. She chides women for their raging vanity, their infinite capacity for self-deception, their idleness, their rapaciousness and folly; men, on the whole, she simply accepts. This may be another of the reasons her books are so socially acceptable in those sections of society least open to change. Women are accustomed to criticism; to being berated, in fiction, for their faults. Men are, quite simply, not. They like to be heroes.

That is quite enough of this letter. If I write too much at any one time the personal keeps intruding, and I am writing a letter of literary advice to a young lady, albeit a niece, on first reading Jane Austen, not a diatribe on the world's insensitivity to her aunt's various misfortunes, or the hard time women have at the hands of men: a fact liberally attested to up and down the streets of the City of Invention.

Alice, I see in your postscript, to my alarm, that you plan to write a novel as soon as you have the time. I sincerely hope you do *not* find the time, for some years to come, for reasons I will go into if and when you reply to this letter, but to do with your age and your apparent unacquaintance with the City of Invention. If you plan to build here, you *must* know the city. I comfort myself that to do a course in English Literature *and* to accomplish any serious writing of your own are commonly held to be mutually exclusive. We know you are doing the one, so the other seems (thank God) unlikely, at least for the time being.

With best wishes,
Aunt Fay

A terrible time to be alive

Cairns, November

My dear Alice,

Just the very fact of existence is amazing: let alone grasping it and weaving it into patterns, as the novelist does. Fashioning nets, as I see it at the moment, to sustain and support the reader as he falls helplessly through the chaos of his own existence – like some wretched passenger flung from a disintegrating plane. You must forgive a certain overexcitement, Alice, in my prose – I have just finished writing a novel, and the sensation is wonderful; as wonderful as when guests, however much loved and welcomed, actually Go Away. Real life, dimly remembered, returns, for good or bad, and it is wonderful.

I look around the hot, dangerous beaches, and into the slow, warm seas where the brilliant fish dart and hover, and the stone fish wait to kill you with a touch, and wonder what I am doing here; and I long for the mists and grey-green grass of England and a landscape altered by human regard, not indifferent and impartial, as are these vast Australian wastes. You may see me soon.

Thank you for your letter. I hope you have already received the £500. I wired it at once. I think it was my bad luck, rather than my wrong judgment, to discover that you had actually read 'The Hound of Heaven'. I suppose I can trust you to tell the truth? Your mother, as I remember, never told a lie: she did not have sufficient memory or consistency of vision to enable her to get away with untruths, as I always could. You will, you say, use the money to buy a word-processor. But, Alice, the machine will not write your book. *You* will still have to do it. You have the fantasy, held by many script editors the world over, that if only you could feed in characters and plots and a variety of adjectives, out would come a book. You might well get a book, but who would read it? Perhaps if you left a key or so out for the Muse (descending, as she tends to, at dawn or dusk) to strike, all would yet be well?

How else but by invoking the Muse, to understand the writing of a novel? I can't imagine, myself, how it's done. Sometimes, it's true, I see the novelist as someone who drops a plumb-line down into the well of the collective unconscious and fishes up God knows what, cleans it up and guts it and serves it up for the reader's dinner. But mostly, I can see only the Muse, leaning over the writer's shoulder, prodding with a bony finger, and bidding him or her write, damn you, write. The Angel in the House is there, too, if you're a woman. Virginia Woolf described her in 'Professions for Women' which she wrote in 1931:

> You may not know what I mean by the Angel in the House. . . . She was intensely sympathetic. She was immensely charming. She was utterly unselfish. She excelled in the difficult arts of family life. She sacrificed herself daily . . . she never had a mind or a wish of her own. . . . And when I came to write I encountered her with the very first words. . . . She slipped behind me and whispered, 'My dear, you are a young woman. . . . Be sympathetic: be tender: flatter: deceive: use all the arts and wiles of our sex. Never let anybody guess that you have a mind of your own.

The Angel in the House stood at Jane Austen's elbow, that is my guess, and she never quite learned how to ignore her – except perhaps in the early *Lady Susan*, for the writing of which, I imagine, she was gently chided by her family, and drew back quickly as at the touch of a cold, cold hand, and never tried that again. But she learned how to get round the Angel, how to soothe her into slumber and write while she slept. Virginia Woolf never quite managed it, in her fiction at least. She abandoned herself to the subtleties of language, and the nuances of response; full of female art and wile; yet died by her own hand one morning, because the world was so dreadful and cruel a place. She knew it, but perhaps saw, as an earlier generation did, art as a retreat from life and not a response to it. I am not condemning, merely observing.

Be that as it may, the air behind the writer is crowded, as the pen moves on. (Don't type, Alice, if you persist in your insane literary plan: use a pen. Develop the manual techniques of writing, so that as the mind works the hand moves. If God had meant us to type, we'd have had a keyboard instead of fingers, etc.)

There's the Muse and this Jungian fisherman (both of whom I invoke, of course, to take charge), but there are also the personifications of every abstract concept there ever was, all shuffling and nudging for the writer's attention, never quite focused, but always there, looking over the shoulder. Truth, Beauty, Love, Justice, Drama – all requiring attention, each trying to claim characters and sentences for their own, filling the air with phantasmagoric howls and moans of complaint and dissatisfaction.

Those are only the ones who stand behind. More real and yet more alarming figures stand in front. ('And those behind cry "Forward", and those in front cry "Back!"') Critics, colleagues, friends whispering insults and exhortations, bearing tales of loss and envy, and a bank manager or so, too, rubbing his hands; and if you're me, children, breaking through the thin walls between idea and experience, the concentrated world of invention and the more diffuse one of reality, saying when is supper ready? Who's going to take me to school? And if all else fails, why then the cat will come and sit on the manuscript. (The cat, I do believe, is the Familiar of the Angel in the House.) Out of all this busy-ness in an empty room – where the writer sits allegedly alone with pen and paper (and *not*, Alice, a word-processor) comes the energy of creation, comes the House of the Imagination, with its charming rooms, its exciting corridors; its locked doors, with the keys hanging where least expected, waiting to be opened by the visitor.

I do believe it is the battle the writer wages with the real world which provides the energy for invention. I think Jane Austen waged a particularly fearful battle, and that the world won in the end and killed her: and we are left with the seven great novels. I know you've been told six. But she did write another, *Lady Susan*, a diverting, energetic and excellent novel, when she was very young, at about the same time as she wrote the comparatively tedious and conventional *Sense and Sensibility* (please don't read it first). She put *Lady Susan* in a drawer. She did not attempt to have it published; nor, later, did her family. My own feeling is that they simply did not like it. They thought it unedifying and foolish, and that wicked adventuresses should not be heroines, and women writers should not invent, but only describe what they know. They had, in fact, a quite ordinary and perfectly understandable desire to keep Jane Austen respectable, ladylike and unalarming, and *Lady Susan* was none of these things.

I will write more of this later. You must understand, I think, the world into which Jane Austen was born. I do not think the life or personality of writers to be particularly pertinent to their work. I know many writers (especially poets) who are boring and conventional as people, yet who produce the most lively and un-ordinary work, and some very intelligent and entertaining writers (as people) who produce work that is singularly dreary.

But I do think *the times* in which writers live are important. The writer must write out of a tradition – if only to break away from it. You must know how to read a novel, for example, before setting out to write one; you must comprehend that they have stories and characters and plots and conversations, and that all these must work to a given end. You must understand that they are meant to be *read*, and that meaning must be absorbed through the eye, and that the ear cannot help. You could, I suppose, work these things out from first principles: but the novel form has developed through centuries and requires a reader more or less as cultivated as the writer. He, or she, writes out of a society: links the past of that society with its future; he or she can demonstrate to the reader the limitations of convention, as Jane Austen did in *Northanger Abbey*, or Thackeray in *Vanity Fair*. The reader may well have mistaken the fictional convention for life itself, so severe is the social indoctrination to which we are all subjected, whenever and wherever we live, and needs to be reminded from time to time that novels are illusion, not reality. Writers seem more conscious of what is going on than those many readers who will quarrel with the content of a novel, but not doubt the whole concept of *the novel*.

I have no doubt, Alice, that you have a set of unquestioned beliefs. I could even give you a brief run-down of your opinions, without ever having met you. You believe, for example:

1. It is better to be good than bad.
2. It is better to be nice than nasty.
3. It is better to be sexually experienced than innocent.
4. Knowledge is good and ignorance bad.
5. White sugar is bad for you, brown isn't.
6. Babies should be picked up when they cry.
7. The strong have a duty to the weak.
8. Cinema is a Good Thing and TV bad.

9. Smoking damages your health.

10. The BBC has the best TV service in the world.

– and so on and so forth. You say, but of course, these things are observably true. This is the world we live in, this is life. But if you investigate yourself, observe what lies beneath the lip service you pay to these notions – for notions they are – you may well discover a layer of yourself that believes quite the opposite. Then what will you do? Stay quiet, I imagine. It takes great courage and persistence to swim against the stream of communal ideas. The stream itself is so much part of daily existence, it is hard to see it for what it is, or understand that it flowed in quite a different direction in other decades.

Jane Austen concerned herself with what to us are observable truths, because we agree with them. They were not so observable at the time. We believe with her that Elizabeth should marry for love, and that Charlotte was extremely lucky to find happiness with Mr Collins, whom she married so as not, in a phrase dating from that time, to be left on 'the shelve'. She believed it was better not to marry at all, than to marry without love. Such notions were quite new at the time. It surprises us that in her writing she appears to fail to take the pleasures of sex into account, but that was the convention at the time: we disapprove, where her society most approves. She is not a gentle writer. Do not be misled: she is not ignorant, merely discreet: not innocent, merely graceful. She lived in a society which assumed – as ours does – that its values were right. It had God on its side, and God had ordained the ranks of His people; moreover, He had made men men and women women, and how could a thing like that be changed? It is idle to complain that Jane Austen lacked a crusading zeal. With hindsight, it is easy to look at the world she lived in, and say she should have. What she did seems to me more valuable. She struggled to perceive and describe the flow of beliefs that typified her time, and more, to suggest for the first time that the personal, the emotional, is in fact the *moral* – nowadays, of course, for good or bad, we argue that it is political. She left a legacy for the future to build upon.

I want you to conceive of England, your country, two hundred years ago. A place without detergents or tissues or tarmaced roads or railway trains, or piped water, let alone electricity or gas or oil;

where energy (what a modern term) was provided by coal, and wood, and the muscle of human beings, and that was all. Where the fastest anyone could cover the ground was the speed of the fastest horse, and where, even so, letters could be posted in London one evening and be delivered in Hereford the next morning. Because people were so poor – most people – they would run, and toil, and sweat all day and all night to save themselves and their children from starvation. Rather like India is today. If you were a child and your parents died, you lived on the streets: if you were a young woman and gave birth out of wedlock you would, like as not, spend the rest of your life in a lunatic asylum, classified as a moral imbecile. If you tried to commit suicide to save yourself from such a life, you would be saved, and then hanged. (These last two 'ifs', incidentally, applied as recently as fifty years ago.) If you stole anything worth more than £5 you could be hanged, or transported to a penal colony for life. If it was under £5 there were long, harsh prison sentences in unspeakable prisons, and the age of criminal liability was seven. No casual vandals or graffiti writers then.

Child, you don't know how lucky you are. If you cheat on the Underground they give you a psychiatrist. If you break a leg, there's someone to mend it. If you have a cold in the nose, you use a tissue and flush it down the W.C.: Jane Austen used a pocket handkerchief, and had a maid to boil it clean. Fair enough, if you're Jane Austen, but supposing you were the maid? You would be working eighteen hours a day or so, six-and-a-half days a week, with one day off a month, and thinking yourself lucky.

If you weren't the maid, you might well be working on the land. Well into the nineteenth century, agriculture was the largest single source of employment for women. And do not think for one moment women of the working classes did *not* work, or had husbands able and willing to support them. A young country girl (and only fifty per cent of the population lived in towns) would be on the farm, cooking, cleaning, washing clothes – and carrying the water, and chopping the wood and lighting the boiler to heat it – feeding animals, milking cows, planting, gleaning, gathering hay. If you worked in the dairy you would at least have the pleasure of developing skills, and would be better paid, but your day would start at 3 a.m. and end in the late evening. Your reward would be in heaven.

The Bible rather rashly claimed that that was where the poor went, thus giving the rich every justification for preserving their poverty. No one's health was good – T.B. afflicted a sizeable proportion of the population. If you, as a young woman, fled to the city to improve your life, you could, with difficulty, become an apprentice and learn the traditional women's trades of millinery, embroidery, or seaming; or you could be a chimney sweep (from the age of six) or you could become a butcher (a nasty trade, despised by men) or a prostitute – 70,000, they reckoned, in London at the turn of the century, out of a population of some 900,000.

Or you could marry.

The trouble was that you had to be able to *afford* to marry. You were expected to have a dowry, provided by your parents or saved by yourself, to give to your husband to offset your keep. For this great reason, and a variety of others, only thirty per cent of women married. Seventy per cent remained unmarried. It was no use waiting for your parents to die so that you could inherit their mansion, or cottage, or hovel, and so buy yourself a husband – your parents' property went to your brothers. Women inherited only through their husbands, and only thus could gain access to property. Women were born poor, and stayed poor, and lived well only by their husbands' favour.

The sense of sexual sin ran high: the fear of pregnancy was great – you might well estimate that half the nation's women remained virgins all their lives. Does that thought alarm and shock you, Alice? Probably, and I dare say rightly. Savage tribes in far-off Africa would never have tolerated it for one moment.

So to marry was a great prize. It was a woman's aim. No wonder Jane Austen's heroines were so absorbed by the matter. It is the stuff of our women's magazines but it was the stuff of their life, their very existence. No wonder Mrs Bennet, driven half-mad by anxiety for her five unmarried daughters, knowing they would be un-provided for when her husband died, as indeed would she, made a fool of herself in public, husband-hunting on her girls' behalf. Politeness warred, as always, with desperation. Enough to give anyone the vapours!

Women survived, in Jane Austen's day, by pleasing and charming if they were in the middle classes, and by having a good, strong working back if they were of the peasantry. Writing was, incidentally, one of the very few occupations by which impoverished and helpless female members of the gentry could respectably – well, more or less – earn money. To be a governess was another, much fabled, occupation. Beautiful and talented governess, handsome scion of ancient housing, marrying where he loved and not where he ought. . . . It was a lovely, if desperate, fantasy. (See Elizabeth and Darcy in *Pride and Prejudice*.)

The average age of puberty, incidentally, was later in their day than it is now. In 1750 we know it to have been between eighteen and twenty. General malnutrition and low female body weights were no doubt the cause. Marriage was later, too: on average between twenty-five and twenty-eight, though Jane Austen's heroines seem to have started panicking in their early twenties. Lydia, in *Pride and Prejudice*, managed it at the age of sixteen, and shocked everyone by revealing everyone's true feelings – trailing her hand with its new wedding-ring out of the carriage window as she rode triumphantly into town, so that everyone would know. Married! Jane Austen herself put on her cap when she was thirty. That is, she announced herself by her dress as out of the marriage market, now resigned to growing old with as much grace and dignity as she could muster. Thirty!

Once you were married, of course, life was not rosy. Any property you did acquire belonged to your husband. The children were his, not yours. If the choice at childbirth was between the mother or child, the mother was the one to go. You could not sue, in your own name. (By the same token at least you could not be sued.) He could beat you, if he saw fit, and punish your children likewise. You could be divorced for adultery, but not divorce him for the same offence. Mind you, divorce was not a way out of marital problems. Marriage was for ever. Between 1650 and 1850 there were only 250 divorces in England.

You put up with the sex life you had, and were not, on the whole, and in the ordinary ranks of society, expected to enjoy it. It tended to result, for one thing, in childbirth. Contraception was both wicked and illegal, against God's law and the land's. Abstinence was the decent person's protection against pregnancy. There were, of course, then as now, libidinous sections of society, the wild young of the upper classes, and free thinkers, who saw sexual freedom as the path to political liberty: and, of course, there were married couples who did find a real and sensual satisfaction in each other – but this was a bonus, not something to be taken for granted: certainly nothing you could go to a Marriage Counsellor about.

The fact that there were 70,000 prostitutes in London in 1801, out of a female population of some 475,000, indicates that your husband at least would not be virginal on marriage. He would quite possibly be diseased. Venereal disease was common, and often nastily fatal.

Alice, by your standards, it was a horrible time to be alive. Yet you could read and read Jane Austen and never know it. And why should you? Novelists provide an escape from reality: they take you to the City of Invention. When you return you know more about yourself. You do not read novels for information, but for enlightenment. I don't suppose Jane Austen thought particularly much about the ills of her society. All this, for her, was simply what the world was like. She would not get upset by it any more than you are upset by the satellites flying across your sky, or the missiles dotted here and there about the earth, pointing instant and ever-ready nuclear death at you and yours. That, you think, is just how it is. You can get used to anything; preferably by mentioning it as little as possible, and using the greater peril to intensify the smaller joy. And good for you!

Now, Alice, there you are, a typical young woman of the 1799s. We're supposing you're working on the land, and of peasant stock. You've scraped your dowry together and you've found your young (or old, often quite old!) man, and got yourself married. Your prime duty is to have children. The clergyman has told you so at the wedding ceremony. 'Marriage is designed by God for the pro-creation of children. . . .' Everyone believes it. (If you turned out to be barren, that was a terrible disaster, not just personally but socially. It made you a non-woman. No infertility clinics then. Just the image of the barren fig tree, blasted by Jesus for what it couldn't help.) But such disasters apart, you're likely to be pregnant within a year of marriage and carry one child successfully to term every two years until the menopause. This seems to be the rate which nature, uninterfered with, decrees for human reproduction. Fifty per cent of all the babies would die before they were two: from disease due to malnutrition, ignorance, or infection. Every death would be the same misery it is today. Your many pregnancies would be plentifully interrupted by miscarriages, and one baby in every four would be still-born. Midwives, mercifully, did not customarily allow imperfect babies to live, nor were they expected to. Child delivery was primitive and there were no analgesics. Child care was not considered a full-time job. Babies were swaddled and hung on pegs out of the way while mothers went on keeping the wolf from the door. If the mother's milk failed, the babies would be fed on gruel, soaked into sacking and sucked out by the baby.

Your own chances of dying in childbirth were not negligible and increased with every pregnancy. After fifteen pregnancies (which meant something like six babies brought to term and safely delivered) your chances of dying were (Marie Stopes later claimed) one in two. Mrs Bennet, giving birth to Mary, must have been worried indeed. Her nerves were bad: she was considered ridiculous, poor thing, for saying so. (I take a very tender view of Mrs Bennet, more tender than her creator does. But I am looking at a society from the outside in, not the inside out.)

Jane Austen herself was the sixth child of a family of seven. Or eight, really. Her mother's second child was epileptic, sent away from home – or presumably, simply not collected from the wet-nurse (more of this later) – and never mentioned again. An older brother, Edward, was reared in a family not his own, where there was more money and more time. Children, coming in large numbers to comparatively few households – as in Ireland today, where contraception is still disallowed – were quite frequently reared in homes better able to accommodate them than their own. Emma, in *The Watsons*, is brought up outside the family, and meets her sisters for the first time when she is a young woman.

Back to you, Alice, mother of six, aged thirty, with your backache and your varicose veins and your few teeth, carrying water from the village well for all your family's needs, and water is about as heavy a soul's task as you can get, and you have to choose if they're going to be clean or you're going to be ill – no, no, start again. I'll elevate you to the gentry, lucky you.

You love your children but your husband owns them, and perhaps you do not love him. If you are unfaithful (and you have many servants and not all that much to do, and gentlemen do not often have occupations but live off inherited wealth and are *about* a lot of the time), he can take your children away from you, to punish you, and very well may. If you are a woman with energy and initiative and knowledgeable friends you will use a contraceptive, a sponge soaked in vinegar, attached to a ribbon. If it doesn't work, there are back street abortionists a-plenty, and death a-plenty too. Mercury is a favourite abortifacient, and useful for curing venereal diseases. The trouble is, the doses that kill foetuses and spirochaete tend to kill their host as well. Oh, bad times! Your lover may, if sufficiently corrupt, use a condom, but the rubber is very thick, very heavy.

So you must understand there were compensations to be found in virginity, in abstinence, in fidelity, and in spinsterhood, which are not found today, and read Jane Austen bearing this in mind.

There were more positive compensations for living in this terrible time. The countryside must have been very, very pretty. The hedgerows and blasted oaks had not been rooted out by agro-industrialists, and wild flowers and butterflies flourished to brighten the gentle greyish greens of the landscape. These days the greens are brighter and the fields are smoother, thanks to insecticides, nitrates and herbicides. And everything you looked at would have been lovely: furniture (if you had any) made of seasoned oak, and by craftsmen working out of a tradition unequalled anywhere in the world – usefulness working in the service of grace. New and different buildings going up everywhere, as the population grew and the middle classes with it, but built in the Italian style of three or four hundred years back. (Go to Florence today, and a terrace you could swear was Georgian turns out to be Renaissance. There's a true culture shock for any members of the cultivated English classes, to whose ranks I am so busily trying to promote you.)

The Bath we know today grew up around Jane Austen's ears, and the proportions which suited the ancient Greeks, and the later Italians, still seem admirable: it is not newness which shocks her successors, in those parts of old Bath newly demolished to make way for the concrete functionalism of new Bath, merely ugliness.

But it's all, I fear, swings and roundabouts. Perhaps landscape, buildings and objects had to be beautiful to compensate for the ugliness of the people. Malnutrition, ignorance and disease ensured a hopping, shuffling, peering, scrofulous population, running short of eyes and limbs. Crutches, peg-legs, glass-eyes and hooks were much in demand. If the children had pink cheeks it was because they had T.B. Do not be deceived by the vision of Georgian England as a rural idyll. Artists of the time liked to depict it as such, naturally enough: (well, except for Cruikshank and Rowlandson who – I hope – went to the opposite extreme) and so did writers, and while you are reading Jane Austen you are perfectly entitled to suspend your disbelief, as she was when she wrote. Fiction, thank God, is not and need not be reality. The real world presses forcibly enough into the imaginative adventure that is our life, without fiction aiding and abetting.

During Jane Austen's lifetime – she was born in December 1775 and died in July 1817 – attitudes, they say,* changed significantly. They became, for a time, before the rigours of Victorian puritanism set in, more relaxed. The age of puberty declined; sexual activity in women was less surprising and less alarming; young women, increasingly, chose to marry for love and not at their parents' choosing. There was an increase in the marriage rates, a lowering of the age of marriage, and a dramatic rise in the illegitimacy rate. Women became more fertile, for good or bad. The rate of infant mortality decreased. The statistics we know: the rest is the kind of sweeping generalization writers of non-fiction love to make, probably more or less true, and good enough for the li. ᴚs of you to pass examinations on the strength of. 'Attitudes' may not have changed: simply, what *happened*, did.

Why, you ask? Better nutrition, a new understanding of hygiene, the aftermath of the French Revolution, the loosening of the stranglehold of the Church, more novels and better novels read by more people in the opinion-forming ranks of society, better poetry – not wide-sweeping social changes, waves in the body politic but the sharp focusing power of individuals – who? Lord Byron? James just-call-me-Steam Stephenson? Blake? Shelley? Jane Austen? The Prince Regent?

Any theory will do until the next one replaces it. Being a writer, I like the better-novels theory, which I hereby give you. If the outer world is a mere reflection of the inner one, if as you refine the

*Mind you, they'll say anything. Do remember.

person so the outer aspects of the world are refined, so will social change work from the inside out, from the individual out into the wider community. Enlighten people, and you enlighten society. How's that?

That is enough for now. I had a letter from your mother. She has not written to me for many years. I fear she may think I am an unsettling influence on you: I know your father feels that feminists (as non-feminists regard me) are dangerous to the structure of society in general and marriage in particular, and does not want the women in his family to have too much truck with me, and the arrival of the £500 will have set too many cats amongst too many pigeons, but I am being as responsible and informative and helpful as I can, so do reassure your mother, and if you care to bring the subject up, your father.

With love,
Aunt Fay

A training in docility

Cairns, December

My dear Alice,

We clearly cannot go on if I don't give you the broad outline of Jane Austen's life. I was brought up, as were many of my generation, with a vague knowledge of how and where she lived, and a general association between her and elegant Regency Bath, all dandies, coaches, balls, finery and elopements. The child's view of history. But I must assume that your knowledge is even vaguer than was mine: you tell me you belong to a Women's Studies Group so I daresay what you *do* know about Jane Austen is that she was *not* the first woman novelist of any note, but merely the first history cared to acknowledge. Well, that's something.

On 16 December (your cousin Tom's birthday) Jane Austen was born at Steventon Rectory in Hampshire. Her father George was the clergyman there. She was the seventh of eight children, and born when her mother was thirty-six. This was not, for those days, a particularly large family. The Austens were energetic and intelligent people, and all their children survived. The second son, however, was born epileptic and brought up by a family in the village, as their own: mention of him is seldom made, although he lived to be nearly seventy, longer than many of his siblings. It was a family that valued intellect highly, and I do not think Mrs Austen was of the stuff that martyrs are made. Many books on Jane Austen (and there *are* many, you'll find, for these days there is a Literary Industry much as there is an Agro Industry: the former being to reading as the latter is to farming) seem determined to present Jane Austen's life as a gentle idyll, lived long ago in the days when life could still be idyllic, before Freud made us knowledgeable and Marx made us guilty; and her family as the perfect English family, the model of all that were to come, and to ignore its vigorous and gritty reality. They may have lived in the past but they were as real to themselves as we are to ourselves, and as complex.

The Austen family is usually described as belonging to the gentry: a class of people below the nobility but a little above the new professional classes (doctors, attorneys, merchants and so forth), who lived off inherited wealth, and had servants. The gentry thought well of themselves, and liked to despise the nobility for their rackety ways, and were despised by them, in their turn, for being worthy and boring. But the statistics of the time make a separate division for clergy of the churches of England and Scotland, and number them as 18,000 (out of a population of 11,000,000), numbering 'nobility and gentry' as a mere 5,000, and certainly not including the clerical classes.

The Austen family was well-read, lively and far from boring. They lived closely together, as was customary at the time, and with evident affection. (But I don't know how you, Alice, would put up with living in your mother's household all your life?) And that is what Jane Austen had to do, and assumed she would do, unless she married. Respectable women in those days did not live by themselves, unless widowed, and even then would be expected to move into the household of a relative, if practicable. The old were not doomed, as they so often are these days, to live alone.

Steventon seems a remote place even today, when the roads are good and there are petrol engines to get you about. It is ten minutes or so drive from Basingstoke, through pretty, wooded countryside. There is nothing *there*, these days, except more woods, and more fields, and a single large, empty, crumbling Victorian house and the charming church opposite it, where George Austen used to preach, and a vast and benign yew tree outside it. The rectory where the Austens lived was pulled down in the 1940s, for reasons not clear to anyone. There is nothing there *now*: certainly no discos, no public halls, no public telephone. I imagine there was very little *then*: the population of Steventon in 1840 was a mere 197 inhabitants, according to a gazetteer of that date, and there is no reason to think it would have changed much since the Austens were there. 'The living is a rectory, valued at £11 4s 7d. The manorhouse has a very antiquated appearance, and bears evident marks of former grandeur,' says the gazetteer. Nevertheless, paradoxically, I think two hundred years ago Steventon would have seemed less isolated than it does today. It is only fifty-eight miles from London. Whitchurch, the nearest market town, was six-and-a-quarter miles to the west, and such a distance that was then considered easily walked. The country gentry were not afraid of the discomfort of travel – they visited often, by trap, coach or carriage – to stay with friends and family, or simply touring and sightseeing.

Nor were the Austens cut off from world events. Their newspapers were informative, intelligent and discursive. It is true that the world of politics and power, dissent and revolution, feature almost not at all, in Jane Austen's novels, but this was surely from choice rather than from ignorance. The motherless son of Warren Hastings, the disreputable governor of India, was brought up in the Austen household for a time, although before Jane's birth. A cousin married a French aristocrat who was beheaded in their Revolution. The young men of the family went off to war. She knew enough, more than enough.

But you must understand that political awareness, let alone action, was not as easy to come by or act upon as it is today. There was no such thing as a Parliamentary Labour Party, no Conservative Headquarters, no Friends of the Earth, or Action for the Low Paid, or Age Concern – no pressure groups to join to stop this or start that. The Church preached acceptance: the working out of God's will here on earth: the general feeling was that since everyone was going to Heaven or Hell, according to their just deserts, what happened down here was on the whole irrelevant. Charity helped the souls of the charitable: that was its point. The filling of the stomachs of the poor with Charity Soup (made from bones and cabbage) was a by-product of the activity. The poor, the gentry felt, had an unfair head-start in the race to Heaven, anyway. Jesus had said they'd get there first, no matter what. Science assumed a gentle progress in the unravelling of the secrets of the universe, and the eventual abolition of ignorance, and with it the end of social ills.

It would have been startling had Jane Austen shown herself 'socially aware' in the modern sense; that she was not can scarcely surprise, or be a matter for condemnation. She was in fact socially aware in the Georgian sense – that is, in a world only recently emerged out of barbarity, however poetic, she analysed and refined still further the new refinement in human discourse: the new interest in the underlying morality, the *real* not the religious morality, of the way people talk to each other, behave to each other, love or don't love each other, and so on. She condemned and she approved; and she took it upon herself to do so, out of no authority other than that invested in her by the worldly judgments of the Austen family, and the power of her own thought, her own moral courage and, simply, her opinion. That, for any writer, is surely more than enough to be going on with.

As children were born into the Austen household they were put out to nurse in the village. That is, other women than their mother would breast-feed them. It was customary at the time. It may or may not have been traumatic for the developing infant – you will have to consult with your pro-and-pre-and-neo-and-anti-Freudian friends. (I imagine most will be anti. It is not these days fashionable to see the self as neurotic, merely society. Twenty years ago the opposite was true. 'People are getting nastier, society nicer': Discuss.) Wet-nursing was a useful way for a peasant woman, especially one who had just lost a nursing infant, or had a still-birth, to earn extra money: it enabled the women of the gentry to preserve their strength and their status as spiritual beings. I was going to add *and* their figures, but I do not honestly believe this entered into their heads: into that of the ladies of the nobility, no doubt, and dwellers in the *demi-monde*, but not, I scarcely imagine, into the head of Mrs George Austen, mother of eight, wife of the Vicar of Steventon and Deane, and her like. She would have had worthier and profounder and more sensible ambitions.

So far as parenting* in England was concerned, until as recently as just after the last war, it was considered enough for the mother (if only by proxy) to look after the child's physical needs and the father to see that it got an education – that the child had emotional needs was not part of the general awareness. The mother's duty was to the father, not the child, if a conflict of interest arose. In the days of the Empire, women followed their husbands around the globe, and shipped their children back to England to live in unspeakable boarding schools, where they were as like as not sexually abused, beaten, and starved, without apparent alarm to anyone. You do not know, little Alice, how recent or how lucky you are.

In the last war, when I was a child, evacuees were shipped out of London schools to avoid Hitler's bombs; working-class mothers

*An American term, I'm sorry. But it has a precise and valuable meaning.

would arrive at the school gate to find their children gone, with no forwarding address. Middle-class women, who organized the evacuation procedure, and who took the separation of child from mother for granted, and their husbands, who felt that for a boy to be made a man of he had to be parted from the mother as soon as possible, simply could not understand the fuss these women made. But then a psychiatrist named Bowlby, in the mid-fifties, wrote about the trauma of mother-child separation so forcibly that he terrified a whole generation of middle-class women into clutching their children's hands every minute of their dependency, and even into discarding prams, because the use of these vehicles entailed separation. John Bowlby is now castigated as being part of the plot-against-women, and may in a sense be so, but at least the child is known to have feelings. We have to be *told* these things, you know. It is surprising how ignorant we are, if we rely on instinct. 'Instinct' usually just means our conditioning to believe this or believe that, without thinking to investigate.

When Jane Austen was ready to be weaned – at perhaps a year old – she would be removed from her wet-nurse, the woman she must regard as mother, and put back into her family. No doubt they were kind to her. But a contemporary social worker would shake her head in disapproval and regard it as a Major Life Event of the kind that contributes to an early death in the actuarial studies of insurance companies. Jane's sister, Cassandra, was two-and-a-half years her senior, and tradition has it, had a temper, but no doubt there were servants enough to keep the older child from attempting to smother this sudden new rival. Well, one hopes so.

Your sister Polly is two years your junior, Alice. I seem to remember terrible incidents, when jealousy got the better of your normally sunny nature. You tried to drown baby Polly: she had to have her nose X-rayed, and how your mother worried in case radiation would get her bone marrow! We have no reason to suppose that children then were different from children now, or that they suffered less from the panic of being displaced. We just take better care (if we belong to the new, caring, maternal classes, that is) to save them from it.

When Jane was seven, in 1783, she was sent off with Cassandra to be educated by a Mrs Cawley, the widow of a one-time principal of an Oxford College, and for this reason qualified to teach girls. One wonders why it was necessary: the brothers were educated at home by George Austen, who was a professional tutor, and if it seemed essential that the girls should have a woman's touch, Mrs Austen was the niece of the President of Trinity, which I would have thought was more than equal to being the widow of the Master of Brasenose – but I joke. . . . It was no laughing matter. Cassandra and Jane, the story has it, were miserable. And Mrs Cawley was horrible. She took the girls to Southampton – (why, why?) – where they both became dangerously ill with a putrid fever. Mrs Cawley did not inform the Austens, but a cousin of the girls, a Jane Cooper, also a pupil, fortunately did. The Rev. and Mrs Austen, and Mrs Cooper, came to retrieve their children. Jane nearly died: poor Mrs Cooper, contracting the infection herself, actually did so.

That episode wouldn't look good on the social worker's file either. In fact, to be so traumatized at such an early age might well get you off a criminal charge in later life. . . . But, not abashed, not having the advantage of hindsight, not even, one imagines, believing that their lives and conduct would be put to such unfair scrutiny by succeeding generations – that kind of thing they left to God – the Austen parents sent Jane and Cassandra off to another school in the following year, 1784.

Now, I know the Rectory must have been crowded: although James was nineteen and at Oxford, and Edward, at seventeen, now lived with the rather grand Knight family (who had taken a fancy to him in his early childhood), Henry, aged eleven, and Francis, aged eight, and Charles, only five, were still at home. (Francis and Charles were to be sent off, when they reached twelve, into the navy, a savage, dangerous and fearful place for children.) And I know that Mrs Austen was behaving as mothers of her class and generation did, and I know that bonding is difficult if you don't breast-feed, and so on, and I know that criticizing the way other mothers bring up their children is always easy and usually despicable (most of us do what we can, as mothers, in the light of our own natures), and that to have Cassandra and Jane about might have been the last straw – especially if Cassandra was peevish and Jane disdainful, and father's pet – but even so, even so – well *really*, Mrs Austen!

Jane and Cassandra went to a boarding school at Reading where, to all accounts, they were happy enough, and the lady in charge had an artificial leg made of cork. At the end of a year Mrs Austen took her daughters back (perhaps she thought they were enjoying themselves too much). Now I know that is unnecessarily unkind, but most Austen biographers go to such lengths to interpret all family events as benignly intended, by saintly people, that I was tempted and I succumbed. The Austen family, like any family, then or now, but especially then, wished to present a good face to the world, and did, and should be allowed to preserve it, and I will not prod further. Mrs Austen had her daughters back.

Except, Alice, I am distressed for the child Jane, and for the young woman she became, and the old woman she never was to be: and I am conscious of the little back bedroom next to her mother's large front-facing one, in the ale-house-turned-residence at Chawton where she, in her early middle age, ended her days, and I *wonder*. I think indeed she bowed her will and humbled her soul, and bravely kept her composure, as a good nun in a good convent might, and escaped into the alternative worlds of her novels: and simply because she *was* so good, or did become so, and her self-discipline was so secure, she brought into that inventive world sufficient of the reality of the one we know and think we love, but which I think she hated, to make those novels outrun the generations.

But we are meant to be being factual: not too fanciful. Not whimsical, as the young Jane Austen was accused of being. Francis went off into the navy and the girls came home. Mrs Austen taught them the domestic arts. Don't despise these, Alice. A time in your life will surely come when circumstances confine you to your home, and that time can be usefully, and pleasantly, and creatively spent looking after it, and making up for the years in which you have left furniture unwaxed, and copper unpolished, and put hot, wet cups of coffee down on delicate surfaces. (If we should ever meet, and you should ever do such a thing, expect to be asked to leave. You must learn to respect anything, even if only furniture, in which human care, effort and affection has been invested.) The domestic arts did not mean merely flower arrangements and watercolour painting: they were useful as well as decorative. (Our forbears, of course, did not make the distinction between the two that we do.)

The servants might do the work, but the women of the family would know in detail how it should be done: how a room should be turned out, how a floor scrubbed, how silver cleaned, bed-clothes aired and dried, clothes cared for, and the winter curtains stored when summer arrived. There was a romance, a reverence and a dignity about housework then: I look forward to the day it is revived. It is too easy to believe that because something is traditionally women's work, that it is worth nothing. On the contrary.

The daughters of the house would be taught to regard waste with alarm – to make a patchwork quilt out of scraps of fabric, a summer pudding out of stale bread and blackberries from the hedgerows. When there were so many shivering, starving wretches around, waste must have seemed not just immoral, but unlucky: an insult to the Gods.

The girls would learn how to sew: they would start with samplers, perfecting different embroidery stitches, on coarse linen. (Your mother and I had one in our bedroom at home when we were children, framed and hanging on the wall: 'The days of man are but as dust – Sara Price, her work. 1799: In God we Trust.' It used to worry me. What use was it, her trusting God? Poor little Sara Price, dead and gone, for all her prayers, all her pious thoughts and all her endeavours. I used to annoy your unfortunate mother by weeping for Sara Price, and being discovered doing so, thus laying unfair claim to a greater sensibility than she.)

The domestic arts included cookery. The girls would not have cooked themselves, but could have instructed and supervised the cook. They would know how a goose should be plucked and dripping clarified, and when the carrots were ready for the gardener to pull. They would know how to clear coffee, by pouring off a little from the jug into a saucer, letting it cool, and then pouring it back into the jug, so the cooler liquid sinks to the bottom, taking the grounds with it. They would know how to make hens lay in the winter time, by removing the rooster from the flock and giving the birds a little chopped meat daily. Their knowledge of the way things grow, and prosper, and work, and are best looked after would be, I imagine, very much superior to yours, Alice. The 'domestic crafts' nowadays taught in schools (and taught to the dullest girls, at that, so I don't suppose *you* ever learned any) are just a sorry hand-me-down from the days when these skills were sharp, necessary and highly regarded.

They do say that the reason for the decline in English cooking, so that for a period of about a hundred years, from the middle of the last century to the middle of this, English cooking was the worst, the wateriest, and the dullest in the world, was due to the social aspirations of the new socially mobile working class; no household could be without its maid-of-all-work, if only living in the cupboard beneath the stairs. The new-style mistress not only felt cooking to be beneath her, but did not have the knowledge or the will to instruct the wretched slattern she employed to do it. The traditions of good cooking, the understanding of food, died out. In the rest of Europe, which remained predominantly rural, and where the population growth was not so sudden and severe as it was in Britain, the traditions were retained.

Well, we learned. We read books. In the last twenty years cookery books have headed the bestseller lists. We got our skills back. They say that in the English private household today the food is better, not just than it used to be, but than almost anywhere else in the world. (Mind you, they'll say anything.) And not so long since my mother, and your mother's mother, took a job in a restaurant and her first task when she got there at eight in the morning was to put the cabbage on for lunch.

I have no doubt that in the Austen household the gardener would bring in a good cabbage during the morning: the vegetable would be soaked briefly in salt water to bring out the slugs, it would be finely chopped immediately before cooking, put into boiling milk (which removes the sulphur and makes it more digestible) until tender, then well drained and served at once. Delicious! as I would have said, in my advertising days.

So much for the domestic arts. Meanwhile, Cassandra and Jane's minds were being elegantly and gracefully developed. Their father taught them the classics, as he, being a clergyman, was well qualified to do. Not so long, after all, since Latin was the written language of all Europe, and its native tongues merely the vernacular. Now there was true internationalism! You will have been taught to reject Latin as irrelevant, elitist, and old-fashioned, but it makes the student alert to the structure of language itself, and more sensitive to the patterns of his own thought. Subject, object, genitive, passive, active – I expect it sounds boring to you, but to me, and to many people of my generation who later became writers, the study of Latin is remembered with pleasure, almost affection. There is no reason to think it was otherwise with Cassandra and Jane Austen – two bright girls.

I am sure that they behaved well. Village girls romped with boys, tumbled in haystacks, laughed aloud, wept freely, argued hugely – but not the clergyman's daughters. Mr Austen wrote to Francis, away at the Royal Naval Academy, when he had finished his training as an officer and was about to go to sea, at the age of fourteen, in these terms:

> I think it necessary, therefore, before your departure, to give my sentiments on such general subjects as I conceive of the greatest importance to you. . . . You may either by a contemptuous, unkind and selfish manner create disgust and dislike: or by affability, good humour and compliance, become the object of esteem and affection: which of these very opposite paths 'tis your interest to pursue I need not say.

A modern father, I daresay, knowing his son was setting off to sea at a time when England was at war with France, when the ships were hell-holes, sailors had to be forcibly enlisted into the navy, and disease and harsh treatment carried off more good men than the French ever did, would have written differently. Never mind. The Rev. Austen preached survival by good manners, and it was not such a bad path to be required to follow. Francis became an Admiral.

The Austen family were very *English*. They did not make a fuss: nor did Jane, in particular, in her novels. The Reverend Austen knew well enough the dangers his son was facing: Jane knew well enough the disease, hunger, and distress that afflicted the village. But the human spirit was supposed to rise above these things, above the dreadfulness of the life of the flesh, outside Heaven but not quite in Hell, and did. It is a mistake, I do believe, to regard their attitude as callous indifference. It was policy. It was the best that could be done, given the general dreadfulness of the world. English middle-class women, still, make less noise in childbirth than anyone else, anywhere in the world. They apologize, saying, 'I'm sorry to make such a fuss, doctor. I'm sure there are others far worse off than me.' What a tradition – wonderful, absurd and dangerous!

And Francis, as midshipman (did you ever see the original *Mutiny on the Bounty* with Charles Laughton? You'll have got a good picture of a midshipman's life from that), would have eaten well, or at any rate better than the men. Hard-tack and brackish water were flung at those unfortunates; up in the officers' mess the same food might, in the end, after a couple of weeks becalmed, be served to their masters, but on porcelain plates, with white napery and polished silver, and perhaps it was the more nourishing for it. There is the spirit, you know, Alice, as well as the flesh. Next time you're in McDonald's, remember it.

So here is the Austen household in the last years of the eighteenth century, busy, cheerful, and self-disciplined, practising compliance and the filial arts. If Jane Austen, in her letters, is occasionally quite remarkably disagreeable, it is hardly surprising. More of this later. She was very bright, very perceptive, lived for ever under her mother's thumb, loving and admiring a father who in the event did her no favours – like Mr Bennet in *Pride and Prejudice* he left his wife and children unprovided for – and lived chastely, though having a sensuous, responsive and romantic nature.

In your language, I imagine, one would describe her as 're-pressed' but that would be an over-simplification; and perhaps imply too strongly that her writing was a reaction to her life, her talent a form of neurosis, and so forth. The initial ability to 'write' is a gift, a talent, a golden present from a fairy godmother: the development of the craft of writing to such a high pitch that the world sits up and takes notice, if sufficiently obsessive, may I suppose be called neurotic, but I say so grudgingly.

She is neurotic.

You are nervy.

I am perfectly normal, thank you.

Writing is an odd activity – other people have occupations, jobs; the writer's life is work, and the work is the life, and there can be no holidays from it. If the pen is not working, the mind is thinking, and even as you sit and watch *E.T.* 'the extraterrestrial', the un-conscious (collective *à la* Jung or personal *à la* Freud) ponders on. Even in sleep you are not safe: dreams pertain to life, and life to dreams, and both to work. There can be no time off, no real diversions, because wherever you go you take yourself; and no pure experience either, unsullied by contemplation, or by the writer's habit of standing back and observing what is going on – which writers will vehemently deny they do, because it sounds passionless, and calculated, but is not. They must observe with the Martian's eye, that of a stranger in a strange land, and marvel at this and be horrified at that, while yet knowing they are part of it, and as prone to human error as anyone. They must develop the link between the mind that thinks, and the hand that writes, until words are contemporary with thought, and even precede it: until the language, as they say, has a life of its own. Language you can allow to have this life but of the other contents of a book – characters, story, purpose – the writer must remain in control. Fear the work of a writer who says, it is my characters who lead me, they take off! They well may, but who will want to follow? It is the writer's *mind* the reader wants: a controlled fantasy, very, very, rarely, the meanderings of an idle author.

The instinct to develop the craft, given the gift, is strong. Jane Austen wrote her first book when she was fourteen. It is entitled *Love and Freindship*, wrongly spelt, and is very funny. She has clearly read many novels: (well, we know she had. Burney, Richardson, Sterne, Fielding – no mean novelists – and no doubt a host of lesser ones too). She mocks the convention. Her characters swoon and run mad:

> What first struck our eyes – we approached – they were Edward and Augustus – Yes, dearest Marianne, they were our husbands. Sophia shrieked and fainted on the ground. I screamed and instantly ran mad. We remained thus mutually deprived of our senses some minutes and on regaining them were deprived of them again. For an Hour and a quarter did we continue in this unfortunate situation – Sophia fainting every moment and I running mad as often . . .

Love and Freindship is written in the form of letters, as was *Lady Susan* later. It was a popular form of fiction at the time, presently to fall into disrepute, for no really good reason. Such a novel has the power of one written in the first person, and the limitations thereof divided by the number of letter-writers the author chooses to involve. A direct authorial voice has to be done without, but the point of view can be from more than a single character. It is not so bad a way of telling a story. To accomplish a letter-novel success-fully requires a special skill, the skill of a born dramatist – the knack of moving a plot along through the mouths of the pro-tagonists, and laying down plot detail, as it's called, without apparently doing so: the body has to be fleshed, but the bones not allowed to show. Jane Austen, even at the age of fourteen, could do these things wonderfully well. The pattern of her storytelling is the same as TV dramatists use today; each letter a new scene, to move the action on, each taking a different viewpoint. Her own anima-tion, her own pleasure in her own skill, shines through the text. She must have found great pleasure in writing *Love and Freindship*, and greater satisfaction in finishing it. The inner excitement, when a writer realizes for the first time that this whole new world of invention and meaning lies waiting to be explored, is intense and overwhelming and exhilarating. It is like falling in love. The feeling of being singled out, of suddenly discovering that you are different from other people, and in some way special, is powerful. What to some non-writers is seen as easy ('I'd write a book too myself if only I had the time') and to others as hard ('I don't know how you do it, I really don't'), to the newly fledged writer is neither easy, nor hard, but simply miraculous. Perhaps it just is that books, novels, loom larger in the lives of writers than they do in the lives of ordinary people, so that to actually *be able to write a book* seems far, far superior an achievement to the novice writer than, say, making a million pounds or inventing a cure for cancer, or marrying the Prince Regent.

Be that as it may, I don't suppose her family allowed her to become conceited about *Love and Freindship*. They will have cut her down to size with gentle mockery – of the same kind that Jane Austen likewise used, and sometimes not so gentle: safe enough on the page, but devastating in real life.

Alice, that is enough for today. I am going to the Qantas office here in Cairns to see about my ticket home. Cairns is a pretty place, but it isn't where I belong. Many of the houses here are built on stilts, incidentally, for reasons as varied as the people who tell me why. Some say it's because of the crocodiles, or the white ants, or because they've always been like that, or for ventilation, or because of the floods, or to raise them above the swamp, or all the better to see the abos from, and some are joking and some are not: hard to tell, so laid back, handsome, sunburned and droll are these Queenslanders. The town itself has wide streets and low wooden buildings, and a branch of David Jones, the department store, made of plywood, with a restaurant where they serve seamen (it's a port, did you know, do you care, do you have a map?), enormous meals of sausages, beans and steak and fried bread and hot sweet tea. The tribal Aboriginals outside in the desert live on wichetty grubs and a nut or berry or so, and blend better into the background, as thin as the white men in the towns are fleshy. Here rich landowners import Asian girls as wives. The girls are glad enough, they say, to escape the hunger and poverty of their own lands; and I have seen them come into town, on occasion, seeming happy and grateful enough, gliding along just behind their striding, paunchy, well-satisfied husbands. Are we to disapprove? I suppose so. But think back to *Pride and Prejudice*. Charlotte Lucas found happiness with Mr Collins, in spite of marrying him for all the wrong reasons. It did for her: it would not do for Elizabeth, who was shocked at first, and heartily disapproved, and then re-thought the whole matter.

I suppose what has happened is that there in Georgian England we had the microcosm of what was to explode into the wide, wild world. Then it was the village girl, whose face was her fortune, obliged to marry the old, rich man from fifty miles away, in order to survive. Now it is the pretty girl from Java who marries the rancher from North Australia.

The population of the British Isles today is some 60 million. In 1800 it was estimated at 11 million. Would you like a break-down of the population, as a parting educational shot? I daresay you dread my return, you are afraid you will actually have to *meet* me, but I assure you, you don't.

Nobility and gentry	5,000
Clergy of the churches of England and Scotland	18,000
Ditto dissenters of every description	14,000
Army and militia, including half-pay, etc.	240,000
Navy and marines	130,000
Seamen in the merchant service	155,000
Lightermen, watermen, etc.	3,000

Persons employed in collecting the public revenue	6,000
Judges, Counsel, attorneys, etc.	14,000
Merchants, brokers, factors, etc.	25,000
Clerks to ditto, and to commercial companies	40,000
Employed in the different manufactures	1,680,000
Mechanics not immediately belonging to ditto	50,000
Shopkeepers	160,000
Schoolmasters and mistresses	20,000
Artists	5,000
Players, musicians, etc.	4,000
Employed in agriculture	2,000,000
Male and female servants	800,000
Gamblers, swindlers, thieves, prostitutes, etc.	150,000
Convicts and prisoners	10,000
Aged and infirm	293,000
Wives and daughters of most of the above	2,427,000
Children under ten years of age	2,750,000
	11,000,000

The whole country, you must understand, and using the language of the times, depended for subsistence, and all the conveniences of life, on the labour of less than one half of the total number. Nowadays the whole depend upon the labour of a third of their number.

Your aunt, Fay

The mantle of the Muse

Cairns, January (getting hotter)

Dear Alice,

Well, you can't trust anyone. In an encyclopedia published in 1813 I find in Volume VII, under 'Midwifery', that the age of menstruation in the human female is sixteen, and that to start any earlier is a disorder and should be treated by bleeding: leeches, that is. The symptoms of the disorder are a full face, full breasts, sighing and a warm imagination. Rather like Lydia in *Pride and Prejudice*. I daresay Lydia might have done better with leeches to quieten her down, than to end up with the shifty Mr Wickham. But in Volume XIV, under 'Physiology', I see the age of menstruation given as fifteen. Both are rather different from the figures I gave you in my earlier letter. Between sixteen and eighteen, I said then, firmly, using other people's figures to prove a point I wanted to make. Fiction is much safer than non-fiction. You can be accused of being boring, but seldom of being *wrong*. I mention my error out of conscience and as a general warning that we all (especially me) tend to remember what it is convenient to remember, and forget what we want to forget, and manage to deduce from given facts what we want to propose.

The encyclopedia is delightfully written by wise and intelligent people. The section on 'Midwifery' is a little alarming, it is true. There was a feeling that placentas should be delivered by hand if nature didn't do it at once, but a rather good notion of using the gentle pressure of the midwife's hand to stop the perineum tearing. If any of your friends are into obsessive natural childbirth I will give them full details, but I imagine, and certainly hope, that most of you will be finding life so exhilarating and full you will have decided to have no babies at all, ever, and be queuing up at the sterilization clinics, where fortunately the wait is long, and natural childbirth, the Leboyer method, and other male plots against the labouring female the last matter on your mind.

But let me quote further from the section on 'Midwifery', here in my encyclopedia. We are dealing with puerperal convulsions – still a major reason for death in childbirth today. The cause is high blood-pressure, and the main work of our ante-natal clinics is to detect it, and cure it before labour starts. Otherwise, now as then, the mother goes into convulsions more severe than in epilepsy, 'in regard to deformity suppressing anything the imagination of the most extravagant painter ever furnished', and dies. But the Georgians had their own view of it.

> It is most frequent in large towns, and in those women who lead the most indolent life: hence it is to be found in the first circles of fashion, in preference to others, and there is one grand circumstance which has great influence on its production, that is, a woman's being with child when she should not. Being obliged to live in a state of seclusion from society for some months, perhaps, she reflects and broods over everything which relates to her situation, and which gives her pain: she recollects she is not to enjoy the society of the babe she has borne, but on the contrary will be obliged perhaps to part with it for ever. She is afraid of her situation being known, and that she shall be considered an outcast to society. In this way she will brood in solitude, 'til at last the mere initiation of labour may be sufficient to excite puerperal convulsions.

They could bleed, give opium, pour cold water over the head when the fit came on, break the waters, or dilate the birth canal by hand (another common practice) to speed delivery, but that was all. If the baby came quickly enough the mother might live: otherwise not.

I tell you all this so you don't forget to be thankful that you live now. Doctors then were faced, often enough, with the problem of which to save, the mother or the child. The Church said the baby: the newborn soul must go on, to achieve its chance of redemption: the mother, the older soul, could be left to die and fly, with any luck, to God. But for the most part, it seems, doctors decided where the likelihood of survival lay, and either performed a Caesarean – which inevitably meant the death of the mother, within a day or so – or opened the head of the baby, within the womb, and removed it piecemeal. They were not brutal: they merely did what they could. But it is not surprising that the taste of the female novel-reader, at the time, so often lay in extravagant romance: that they loved wild gothic tales. Every child would be brought up with a knowledge of the closed bedroom door, the hurrying of midwives and doctors, the black bags in which the instruments were carried – the vectis, or the new, safer forceps. 'There is still a query,' says my encyclopedia, which seems to be intended to serve as the only text-book a surgeon would have, 'that if forceps be so much better than the vectis, how is it that the vectis is still in use by some? For no other reason but because it is easier to use: the instrument requires less skill, and for that reason is it preferred by those who have no more skill than they know what to do with.'

Neither Jane nor Cassandra had children. I am not saying that Jane stayed single because she didn't want them, and children were where marriage led. I am just saying she was an imaginative person – and just as an imaginative person has more difficulty than others in learning to drive – the mind forever leaps ahead, constructing possible *scenarios* of death and disaster – so she would have looked ahead into her own life, and not relished the screams, and the pacings, and so forth. Would you have been brave enough, Alice – and why should she be braver than you?

It is only recently that it has become acceptable for a woman to give voice to her quite rational fears of childbirth. She was supposed to keep quiet and get on with it: and certainly not take steps to avoid childbirth by using contraceptives, abstinence or declining to marry. Queen Victoria, a mother of nine, disgraced herself by grumbling publicly about the pain, and referred to childbearing as 'the shadow side of marriage'; and when anesthetics first became available, took chloroform – just a little, soaked into a handkerchief – at the birth of her eighth and ninth child. The country felt rather let down; 'in sorrow shalt thou bring forth' was much quoted at her, but fortunately for the rest of us, she refused to be abashed, and the habit caught on. Nowadays, the woman who declines to have children is still regarded with some (though shrinking) curiosity: her motives are not likely to be nearly as strong, her fears not nearly so basic, as those that must have assailed her female forbears. Namely, the expectation of pain and the fear of death.

But those matters lay ahead for Jane Austen. It was 1790. She was not yet 'out'. That is to say, she had not yet been put on the marriage market: adorned, taken to balls and parties and exposed to the company of suitable young men, in the hope that she would 'catch' one. I am not against such methods of regulating the hearts and lives of young women: it is certainly better that they should fall in love with someone suitable than with someone who, to the older generation, can be seen to be, say, a neurotic bully and a potential alcoholic. I know such observations will annoy you very much: but arranged marriages are normal in great areas of the world today – and the record of the modern West in marriage matters is not so hot. But I can already hear you say 'but marriage is an outmoded institution, anyway, what *is* she talking about....' I'll desist.

Anyway, at the age of fifteen Jane Austen seemed happy enough. She wrote *The History of England* and dedicated it to her sister Cassandra in these terms:

> ... by a partial, prejudiced and ignorant Historian.
> To Miss Austen, eldest daughter of the Revd. George Austen this work is inscribed with all due respect by
>
> > The Author
>
> N.B. There will be very few dates in this History.

The young Miss Austen encompassed three hundred years of England's past in fifteen pages, in a kind of early *1066 and All That*. She shows herself as very clever, very funny, exhilarated and exhilarating and impatient.

> The Events of this Monarch's reign ... (Charles 1st) are too numerous for my pen, and indeed the recital of any Events (except what I make myself) is uninteresting to me.

You see! The born novelist. She is raising invention above description; what she makes herself above what the real world has to offer. She will put up with writing a history so long as she doesn't have to get the dates right, and mocks those who take the whole thing seriously, and so long as she can be biased:

> My principal reason for undertaking the History of England being to prove the innocence of the Queen of Scotland, which I flatter myself with having effectually done, and to abuse Elizabeth, tho' I am rather fearful of having fallen short in the latter part of my scheme –

– and also so that Cassandra – at the time eighteen – could be involved, could illustrate the *History*, in the form of kings and queens, which she did, with evident pleasure, but in a manner which would nowadays be thought to be the work of someone far younger. (She would never, these days, have got to art school.) History, of course, was seen as the story of monarchs; the notion that it concerned the development of society is comparatively new. I doubt that you could reel off the dates of the Kings of England, Alice, as I still can.

In the same year Jane Austen wrote an unfinished novel – *Lesley Castle* – also in the form of letters, but with a bigger cast of letter-writers – and dedicated it to her brother Henry in these terms:

> To Henry Thomas Austen Esqre.
> Sir
> I am now availing myself of the liberty you have frequently honoured me with of dedicating one of my Novels to you. That it is unfinished, I grieve: yet fear that from me, it will remain always so: that as far as it is carried, it should be so trifling and so unworthy of you, is another concern to your obliged humble
>
> Servant – The Author.

> Messrs. Demand & Co. – please pay Jane Austen, spinster, the sum of one hundred guineas on account of your Humble Servant
> £105.   H.T. Austen

There! You see, already conscious that writing is worth money, deserves money, that pleasure for one is work for another, and must be compensated for in financial terms. And *Lesley Castle* was, increasingly, work, as she got herself embedded deeper and deeper into the pit she'd dug for herself; that is, too many characters, and too much peripheral event, and no apparent central drive or purpose – which is why she simply stopped writing it – she'd bored herself.

I hate this kind of cold conclusion; these sweeping assessments of motive with which, in the present, we look back at the past. I despise it in biographers, and yet find I am doing it myself. Put me in a pulpit and I know I too would soon be saying: 'God wants us to do this, that and the other because God means us to be this way, that way or the other way . . .' As if I knew: as if I had a special Hot Line to Him.

Do be warned, Alice. The reason Jane Austen joked about charging Henry one hundred guineas for *Lesley Castle* is as likely to be the result of a frivolous conversation over the dinner table the night before, as to the motive I attribute to her. The reason she stopped writing *Lesley Castle* may have been because she ran out of paper, or shut her thumb in the lych-gate of Steventon Church the previous Sunday: or because she was reading the manuscript aloud to her family one evening and they all started yawning and looking for the cards. There is simply no way of knowing – and I take it back.

But *Lesley Castle* starts marvellously! Little by little the awfulness of this Scottish castle, and the eccentric nature of its inhabitants, emerges: the two Lesley sisters, both very tall, gain a stepmother who is very short. Charlotte Cuttrell, to whom all write in their passion and despair, is an unfeeling audience and, it is evident in her replies, thinks only about food – its preparation and its eating – but by the ninth letter (the one before last) invention is wearing thin, as the postscript to the letter shows:

> I am afraid this letter will be but a poor specimen of My Powers in the Witty Way: and your opinion of them will not be greatly increased when I assure you that I have been as entertaining as I possibly could.

'Well, yes, Jane,' Henry may have remarked, as the family sat beside the fire in the evening, and the servants drove the warming pans into the beds upstairs, and they had finished politely admiring Cassandra's sketches, and talked a little about what was happening in France – that year of the declaration of the Republic and the setting up of the Revolutionary Tribunal – and whether cousin Eliza, who had married a French aristocrat, and a Roman Catholic one at that, would not soon be faced with the penalty of her wilfulness – and then perhaps wondered whether they should send off for Mary Wollstonecraft's *Vindication of the Rights of Women* – and then, when finally Jane had read out her last instalment of *Lesley Castle* (letter 9), 'Well, yes, Jane, you are quite right. It *is* a poor specimen of your powers in the witty way, and I suggest you give up.' Henry would have been nineteen at the time: he was a scholar and at Oxford: hard for any member of a family audience, hearing that postscript read aloud, *not* to make such a remark: and Henry seems the one most likely to make it. He was the joker of the family.

He later, after Jane's death, some twenty years later, when he had sobered down, wrote a preface to *Northanger Abbey* and *Persuasion*, of really acute sycophancy: 'Neither the hope of fame nor profit mixed with her early motives . . .' writes Henry. But oh, Henry, once your sister joked and said she'd charge you a hundred guineas for an unfinished novel – could you have forgotten that? Or even at the time, did you raise your eyebrows, even while you joked, and do your best to discomfit your clever little sister?

Whom not everybody, incidentally, liked. Philadelphia Walter, an Austen relative, wrote in this manner when Jane was twelve:

> Yesterday I began an acquaintance with my two female cousins, Austens. My uncle, aunt, Cassandra and Jane arrived at Mr F. Austen's the day before. We dined with them there. The youngest (Jane) is very like her brother Henry, not at all pretty and very prim, unlike a girl of twelve; but it is a hasty judgement which you will scold me for. My aunt has lost several fore-teeth which makes her look old – [no one knew about calcium then: tradition held it that you lost one tooth with every child, and you probably did. So Mrs Austen would be eight down.] – my uncle is quite white-haired, but looks vastly well: all in high spirits and disposed to be pleased with each other. . . . Yesterday they all spent the day with us, and the more I see of Cassandra the more I admire – Jane is whimsical and affected.

Poor Philadelphia: if she had known the scrutiny this letter was to be subjected to – if she had known how she was to be disliked for daring to criticize Jane – no doubt she would have been more careful in her description. But girls are often at their plainest at twelve, of course, and certainly self-conscious, and in her efforts to impress her cousin with her virtue, Jane may have appeared self-righteous; and with her imagination, whimsical (i.e. given to an irritating irrationality).

But I do dislike all these 'ifs', and 'may haves'; they can only be speculation; and are in a way parasitical: the present sucking nourishment from the past, the living from the dead, as if there wasn't enough emotion and event now to sop up all our desire for analysis and explanation. Jane Austen made a bad impression on Philadelphia Walter, and that's that.

She may (there we go again) have made an unfortunate impression on the young men she met. I suspect she was too clever, too well read, altogether too full of mockery. There is a race of young men abroad today who are fascinated by what we call 'strong' women, women who work, think, earn, have independent habits and who would no more make a man a cup of coffee – unless perhaps he was ill – than they would commit murder; women to whom the personal is the political, and for whom admiration is the most difficult emotion of all, defining men as they do as dangerous at best, and despicable at worst.

That is enough of that. I am going to pack. The temperature here is 32°C. That is very hot. In England, I believe, it is around 8°C. There seems little point in packing, since what little I have here is of even less use there. The manuscript has gone off to the publisher. I had it photocopied in Cairns and sent it off from the Post Office there. Australians do not take the post as seriously as we do. I had difficulty persuading them to put stamps on the package anywhere near sufficient to guarantee its arrival in Sydney, let alone in the UK. They are happy in their isolation, in the hot sun. But *Emma*'s there, in the bookcase: subversive reading, with its lessons in moral refinement.

I have taken a long time getting Jane Austen through her child-hood and adolescence. 'The facts known about Jane Austen can be put in a nutshell', I remember reading in my Matric. English Lit. textbook at school, and wondered at the time why it was thought appropriate to put facts in nutshells. Do you know? It is true there isn't much known: we have such of her letters as her sister Cassandra thought it proper for the world to see, after her death; a few reports from friends and relatives, and, of course, the texts of her books from which, as Seventh Day Adventists do with the Bible, you can deduce pretty much what you wish.

I will fill you in on the rest of her life, in a sentence or two, if not a nutshell, and return to it in later letters. I don't think I will go to pack: I think I will simply lie in the shade by the pool. (The bus driver will take this letter to the post box for me. There is something about this place that reminds me of Georgian England. It is not just the alarming fact that they sentence criminals – those whom they define as criminal: that is, mostly Aboriginals – to prison sentences with hard labour, but that, more positively, simple human needs are recognized and met, with an easy, natural helpfulness, and with the sense that everyone is working together towards the best of all possible worlds.)

Jane Austen did not marry. She had no children. Nor did Cassandra. Jane Austen lived at Steventon until she was twenty-five, when her father retired. The family then went to Bath, where her father presently died. Her mother, Cassandra and she, left unprovided for, then lived by the courtesy of relatives for two years in Southampton, and then in the village of Chawton, in a house which had once been an inn, in the shadow (more or less. It's half a mile away) of the great house where her brother Edward lived in style. In this house she wrote *Emma*, *Mansfield Park* and *Persuasion*. You can still visit the house, and see the small round table where she worked. I went there once and it seemed to me her spirit was still there: the part of her that was the writer, at any rate. You may dismiss this as silly if you like.

In 1817 she died, of, it is now said, Addison's Disease. Then it was described as a lingering illness. She was forty-one.

She was born on 16 December (Sagittarius, and the birthday of my third son). She died on 18 July (the date on which my second son was born). Her books, as they vulgarly but truly say, live on. If writers build well and soundly, and in the service of Truth, who is the God they worship there in the City of Invention, their houses live after them, as a good house in this world remains, long after its occupants have turned to mould. It always seems strange to me, how different families serve shifts in the same house; as if the house owned them, sucked them dry, spat them out and tried again – and not the family that controlled the house at all.

I digress. 'Til the next letter, Alice,

Your aunt, Fay

Pity the poor writer

The Lakeside, Canberra, January

My dear Alice,

I have shipped out of North Queensland and come down to Canberra, before leaving for home. I know it adds a few thousand miles to an already outrageous distance – the world, so small a place to the telephone user (fifteen digits and variations thereupon will these days get you anywhere in a couple of seconds), is truly horrendously large to the person who has to physically move themselves from one part of it to another – but I find I need time before launching myself from the Southern Hemisphere back into the Northern. Therefore Canberra. I create the same distractions for myself – visits to friends, consultations with publishers, TV producers and so on – as I create before embarking on a new novel or play. Some writers classify the delaying process as research, and get advances from publishers and grants from Arts Councils to do it but I (I like to think) know it for what it is, an uneasy mixture of terror, idleness and a paralysing reverence for the Muse which, descending, prevents the writer from putting pen to paper for an intolerable time; till something happens – a change in the weather, an alteration to the pattern of dreams – which makes it possible to begin.

North Queensland lives by its wits and its physique – it gives no credence to writers, especially women; what use imagination when a crocodile advances or the locusts get the sugar-cane? You need a flame thrower and a helicopter, not a novel. Down in Canberra things are very different. It is a city of astonishing artifice and astonishing beauty. Once it was a barren plain, an indentation in the dusty desert: now it is striped by tree-lined avenues – the trees imported by the hundred thousand from Europe, over the years – in pretty, idiosyncratic suburbs where house prices define the status of the occupants, and when you change houses you change your friends, willy-nilly – and dotted by swimming pools, and graced by

tranquil man-made lakes. It is a place of final and ultimate com-
promise: it exists only because Sydney and Melbourne could not
agree where the seat of Australia's government was to be, and so
invented this place, somewhere in between – but rather nearer
Sydney. It has handsome new buildings; a High Court where the
courts are like theatres and judges and criminals play to an
audience; the prettiest, leafiest, and most savagely, suicidally con-
spiratorial university in the world, the ANU – and it has *readers*.

I talked to them last night. I read to them. I read from *Puffball* –
or rather I read *all Puffball*, leaving out the bits difficult to précis.
A potted novel: a Reader's Digest version. Once I was too terrified
to open my mouth in public – my heart raced and my voice came
out in a pitiful mouse-squeak – but now I enjoy haranguing
hundreds.

It is practice, only practice, and learning to despise and put up
with your own fear that works the transformation – which I tell
you, Alice, just in case you suffer yourself from that terror of public
speaking which renders so many women dumb at times when they
would do better to be noisy. And if you are in a Committee meeting
or at a Board meeting or a protest meeting, speak first. It doesn't
matter what you *say*, you will learn that soon enough, simply *speak*.
Ask for the windows to be opened, or closed, or cigarette smokers
to leave, or no-smoking notices to be taken down – anything. The
second thing you say, later, will be sensible: your voice will have
the proper pitch, and you will be listened to. And eventually, even,
enjoy your captive audience.

Here in Canberra, this fictitious place, this practical, physical,
busy, restless monument to invention, they love books and they
love writers. Different cities call out different audiences. In Melbourne the audience is middle-aged and serious; in Sydney middle-
aged and frivolous; here in Canberra they are young, excitable,
impressionable and love to laugh. They want to know: they ask
questions. They nourish you, the writer, with their inquiries, and
you fill them with answers; right or wrong, it hardly matters. It's
always wonderful to find out that there is a view of the world, not
just the world: a pattern to experience, not just experience – and
whether you agree with the view offered, or like the pattern, is
neither here nor there. Views are possible, patterns discernible – it

is exciting and exhilarating and enriching to know it. You need not agree with the person on the platform, but you discover that neither do you have to agree with friends and neighbours: that's the point. You can have your own view on everything – and this, particularly in a place such as Canberra, is liberty indeed. And it is why, I think, increasingly, any seminar on Women and Writing, or Women Writers, or the New Female Culture, or whatever, is instantly booked up – by men as well as by women – and readings by writers, and in particular women writers – are so popular. At last, it seems, there is some connection between Life and Art, the parts *do* add up to more than the whole: we always thought it! We discover – lo! – we are not alone in the oddity of our beliefs. Our neighbour, whom we never thought would laugh when we laughed, actually does.

It puts, of course, quite a burden on the writer, who is expected to direct all this mental theatre, to be seen as an Agony Aunt as well as the translator of the Infinite, and the handmaiden to the Muse, and may not have realized, on first putting pen to paper, where it would all end. But we have our royalties to give us some worldly recompense: our foreign sales, our TV rights, and so on. Like the real Royalty, it does not become us to complain.

Jane Austen and her contemporaries, of course, did none of this. They saved their public and their private energies for writing. They were not sent in to bat by their publishers in the interest of increased sales, nor did they feel obliged to present themselves upon public platforms as living vindication of their right to make up stories which others are expected to read. Imagine Jane Austen talking at the Assembly Hall, Alton, on 'Why I wrote *Emma*'. But times, you see, have changed, and writers have had to change with them. When the modern reader takes up a 'good' novel, he does more than just turn the pages, read and enjoy. He gratifies his teachers and the tax payer, who these days subsidizes culture to such a large extent, in every country in the world; he gives reason and meaning – not to mention salary – to all those who work in Arts Administration and libraries and Literature Foundations, and Adult Education and the publishing, printing and book distribution trades – nothing is simple, you see, nothing: nothing is pure – and by virtue of the pressure put upon the reader to read, the burden of the writer is that much the greater. If your writing has any pretensions to literary merit, you *must* appear, you cannot shelter behind the cloak of anonymity: you have to be answerable, although you would rather stay home knitting, or dipping a horrified toe into the dangerous coral seas of the uncultured North. It won't do: you have to come down to Canberra: you want to come down to Canberra. Somehow, it is registered as duty. You're lucky, moreover, if they pay your fare.

All this you will discover when you finish your novel and it is acclaimed. It is very rare for writers to be acclaimed at an early age, of course, but you will quote Keats and Shelley at me, and I will predictably say, 'poets are different, poets are expected to have a view of their response to the world, and can do *that* from adolescence onwards; novelists are expected to have a view of the world itself,' and you will say, 'not so, why?': and neither of us will believe the other, so I shan't continue on this theme. All I want to say is that a writer's life is not a piece of cake, though better, I swear, than a waitress's. (I was one of those once, too.) And that, if you want to be a writer – don't; if you want to *write*, which is a different matter, nothing will stop you, not lack of time, nor the existence of husband, home or children; these things will merely sharpen your determination, not deter you. And that it is useless looking for things to say; if you have nothing to say, as my mother, your grandmother, used to remark to us girls, shut up. 'Stay silent,' she phrased it, being a lady to her bones. That may have been why our father, your grandfather, left her. A few plain words condemning his drunken fornicating habits might well have stopped them, and him in his tracks. Men – I use the term generically to include the female, as I so often in my letters to you use the male pronoun to include the female – are like children; they tend to misconstrue lack of reproof as lack of interest, as indifference.

I do wonder what it was that led Jane Austen into believing that her novels were publishable: were acceptable to a readership other than that of her immediate family and friends? She wrote the early books, initially, to be read aloud. Her tiny, fine handwriting, lacing the page this way and that – paper was expensive and it was customary to cover every available patch of it with writing – was hardly conducive to actual *reading*. The sense of the books, the delicacy of the language, the phrasing, the dialogue – all was written to be absorbed by the ear, not the eye. This is one of the reasons, of course, why a Jane Austen novel can be so wonderfully read aloud, and pleasurably listened to, on the radio. It is their true, their proper form. And if you have formed a writing style through your early work, it is likely to continue into your later. *Persuasion* was no doubt written with publication in mind – that is, to be absorbed by the eye, through the turning of pages, and a multitudinous eye at that, including all ranks and types of owners – but the early conception of a family audience, gathered round a vicarage fire, or sitting in the sun of a late afternoon, listening, smiling, responding, with evident pleasure, would not easily be forgotten.

And this – the mental presence of an actual audience – is another reason for the peculiarly dramatic scene-setting of which Jane Austen is so fond. She knows how to end a scene, an episode, a chapter, before beginning the next: when to allow the audience to rest, when to and how to underline a statement, when to mark time with idle paragraphs, allowing what went before to settle, before requiring it to inform what comes next.

It is a very modern technique. It requires, bluntly, and in modern terminology, consciousness of audience, and audience reaction. Jane Austen, I surmise, learned hers by reading aloud; listening to the stirrings, sighings and coughings of her audience. Today many writers learn by cutting their teeth on screen or TV or radio plays, before settling down to write novels; and though many who eschew the other forms of writing, and only write novels and are proud of it, will deny a sense of audience, saying, 'But I don't think of the readers at all. I only think of *me*,' when what they usually mean is, 'I am my own reader; I am both writer and reader. I must be the one, to gratify the other.' For without this sense, there can be no pleasure by the writer in the sense of manipulating, through the written and the spoken word, the mind of the reader: and none of the mildly masochistic glory the reader has in being so manipulated and controlled as to actually have feelings he would not otherwise have had, and thoughts likewise, and discover in himself opinions he never knew he held. Truly, Alice, books are wonderful things: to sit alone in a room and laugh and cry, because you are reading, and still be safe when you close the book; and having finished it,

discover you are changed, yet unchanged! To be able to visit the
City of Invention at will, depart at will – that is all, really, education is about, should be about.

But that's enough of that for now. You may observe, that like so
many of my generation, brought up on one side of the great cultural
arts/science divide, I tend to believe that Science Faculties do not
exist.

There is another very boring side to this reader/writer inter-
connection. It happens to writers who offer, or seem to offer, a
solution to moral complexities of life, who do more than just offer
plots and characters. 'There is some mystery here,' the reader
thinks. 'Let us find out what it is.' They send questionnaires. One
arrived this morning, forwarded from England. It comes from a
post-graduate student, doing a thesis on feminist literature. It goes
like this:

1. In adolescence, were your favourite or formative writers
female?
2. Of these early influences, which do you think have been
important to your development as a writer?
3. Who was the first writer or writers you thought of as having a
specifically female point of view?
4. Would you consider them so today?
5. Who would you consider to be the major figures in feminist
fiction?
6. Does the writing of women from other cultures interest you as
a writer?
7. Do you think that there are male writers writing from a point
of view that is sympathetic to feminism?
8. Do you consider that a male writer can write convincingly
about female experience, and if so, who would you give as an
example?
9. Which area of female experience do you think has been most
neglected by writers to date?
10. Do you think that certain female experiences have actually
been suppressed in literature?
11. Are you happy with the teaching of literature in schools?
12. A. Rich has referred to our language as '. . . man-made, inadequate, and lying . . ' Do you think that a feminist vocabulary

(a clumsy phrase, but can't think of a better one) is desirable or
necessary?

13. Why do you think that historically we know much more about
women in literature than in the visual arts?

I will answer the questionnaire, of course, as best I can, and out
of a general courtesy, but I do not think my answering will help the
inquirer understand literature, men, women, or me. I can only
reply as a reader, not a writer. I would have to write a whole play,
or novel, based on the theme of every single question, and she
would have to watch that, or read it, and absorb it, and understand
it, before she would be one jot further on; and then she would have
another questionnaire to send out, based on that, and we would
never, ever finish. Of course we wouldn't! The whole way in which
fiction differs from journalism – a journalist would have no trouble
answering the questionnaire – is that it attempts to reduce the
enormous complexities of the whole to something comprehensible
by an imaginative leap – we are humble sheep in a field of infinity:
behold, a little ditch. Over goes the writer first: the readers follow
after. But it was only such a little ditch. . . . The journalist knows
nothing of this: he has no concept of scale. He will answer question
No. 1 briskly and informatively. He will say, 'my favourite writers
were female but my formative writers male, in adolescence. In my
childhood the position was reversed, and in my adult life I have had
no favourite or formative writers' or something of that kind, and
she will ponder this and, with any luck, will decide it means something. I will be still on Act 1, scene 3, detailing the nature of
adolescence and the sexual desires of an androgynous English
teacher.

These inquiries – mostly from women doing theses on some
aspect of literature and/or feminism today – seem to believe that,
if only they understood the writer, they would then understand the
book. Recognizing that there is something inexplicable about the
work, their ambition is instantly to nail it, and then explain it. Or
perhaps, for some, it is that they are baffled by the writer's ability
to do what they themselves would like to do, but can't. That is,
write a novel that others want to read. They can write essays,
memos, letters – why is it then that they can't write novels: that the
words lie dead and flat upon the page? There is some secret here,

they feel, that the writer knows and unfairly withholds. If only the inquirer digs deep and uncomfortably enough – then the writer will be obliged to divulge the secret, every man can be his own novelist, and never spend a penny on a book again.

I worked in an advertising agency once. We were taken over by rational Americans, who could not bear the risky and expensive waywardness of the way we worked, and pinned us down by research, and tried to nail the creative process, so that successful campaigns could be produced in a rational way – so many positive adjectives here, so many exclamation marks there, a set ratio of copy to picture – but it never quite worked. The success rate was as high if we were guided by instinct as it was if we went by computer and research. Management retired, baffled, and let us get on with it in our own way, losing millions here, gaining millions there, for all the wrong reasons. It is for this same reason, the desire to control the creator and to calculate audience response, that once 'great' TV series decline and fall away; the initial creativity runs out; is drawn off like water from a well, by script editors who rationally apply a formula that 'works'; only the well must presently run dry. Viewers notice it long before script editors: viewing figures fall, and only writers understand why. There is construction here, and description, but no invention. *Dallas* palls, *Upstairs Downstairs* brings a yawn.

Anyway, last night at Canberra the readers and the would-be writers came to hear me speak, and to ask questions. It was a particularly good evening. Speaker and audience animated one another: these occasions, when all goes well, are like nothing else. They are half-way, for the audience, between going to a theatrical performance and reading a book; and for the writer, half-way between the former and writing one. A new art form:

$$\frac{\text{Audience}}{\text{Writer}} \times \frac{\text{Speaks}}{\text{Acts}} = \text{Enlightenment}$$

The phenomenon is not new. Readers and listeners made tracks to Snorri Sturluson, twelfth-century writer of Icelandic sagas, poet, politician and historian. They came, over snow and tundra, by horse and cart and reindeer and sleigh. The questions would have been the same then as they are now. 'Mr Sturluson, do you work regular hours or do you wait for inspiration to strike? Do you take notice of what the critics say? Of what the King says?' (He had better have paid more attention to the latter: he came to a sorry end by the King's hand.) 'What were the early influences on your work?'

Human nature does not change over the centuries. If one writer is born to every five hundred non-writers, so are five critics and ten sceptics, twenty questioners and, thank God, one hundred simple readers: the proportion was the same in the twelfth century as it is today: only the scale is different, and (in the West) there are lighter penalties for writing what displeases, and thinking what is inconvenient. Fiction, on the whole, and if it is any good, tends to be a subversive element in society. Elizabeth Bennet, that wayward, capricious girl, listening to the beat of feeling, rather than the pulsing urge for survival, paying attention to the subtle demands of human dignity rather than the cruder ones of established convention, must have quite upset a number of her readers, changed their minds, and with their minds, their lives, and with their lives, the society they lived in: prodding it quicker and faster along the slow, difficult road that has led us out of barbarity into civilization.

Now, the questions asked last night by the readers of Canberra, those same questions asked of Sturluson and Tolstoy and George Eliot and any writer who even once ventures a public opinion on the way the world is run, and their relation to it, are sensible enough. They are what I ask other writers. They are what I would ask Jane Austen if I were her contemporary. They are the questions that her biographers try to answer for her.

I think they sometimes get it wrong. I look at the small, round table in the house at Chawton at which she wrote *Emma*, *Mansfield Park*, and *Persuasion* and am told that when people came into the room she covered her work and put it aside. They deduce from this (a) that she was ashamed of her work and (b) that it was criminal that she should be disturbed in this way.

Most writers choose to cover their work when someone else comes into the room. They know it does not appear to best advantage out of context. They fear that, taken line by line, it sounds plain foolish. They do not want to answer questions. 'And who is this Mr Knightley I see on the third line down? Is he going to marry Emma?' (I daresay two chapters into the work she simply didn't know, but no reader/visitor is going to believe a thing like that.) So the work is covered. It isn't shame, merely prudence. As for disturbances, some writers thrive on them. For many, if life provides uninterrupted leisure for writing, the urge to write shrivels up. Writing, after all, is part of life, an overflow from it. Take away life and you take away writing.

I would have thought the small, round table, half-way between fire and window, sitting with a warm back and life going on the other side of the pane, when you chose to look up from the page, and the occasional knock at the door, and a putting away of the work, was an ideal place and way for any writer to work. It's how I choose to do it, I know that. I won't have her pitied for it.

I do pity contemporary male writers, who have wives to bring them coffee and answer the phone to the bank manager, and no excuse not to undertake, not to complete, not to get published, and who find themselves with nothing to say. Writers were never meant to be professionals. Writing is not a profession, it is an activity, an essentially amateur occupation. It is what you do when you are not living. It is something you do with your hands, like knitting. We were not born with typewriter keys for fingers; we were born to pick up sticks and scratch away in mud and make our ochre marks on the walls of caves. Now, given that we must make a living, we join the Writers' Guild and the Society of Authors and fight for our rights and our royalties and have to do so – but we should not be misled as to the true nature of our occupation. We do not need offices and a muted typewriter and no disturbance – we need a table half-way between the fire and the window, and the muted sound of the world around: to be of that world, and not apart from it. It is easier for women than it is for men, the world being what it is, and women writers, to their great advantage, are not allowed wives.

Alice, how is your novel? I do quite like your title. *The Well of Loneliness*: but I think someone has already used it. Do check with your tutor. You ask me how to write a 'good novel'. Well, the writers, I do believe, who get the best and most lasting response from readers are the writers who offer a happy ending through moral development. By a happy ending I do not mean mere fortunate events – a marriage, or a last-minute rescue from death – but some kind of spiritual reassessment or moral reconciliation, even with the self, even at death.

'This is a far, far better thing,' said Dickens at the end of *Tale of Two Cities*, 'than I have ever done.' And look how that sold!

Readers need and seek for moral guidance. I mean this in the best and even unconventional sense. They need an example, in the light of which they can examine themselves, understand themselves.

If you are good, Jane Austen promised, you will be happy. Emma learns to control her foolish impulses, and marries Mr Knightley. Anne in *Persuasion* holds fast to her ideals of unchanging love, and brings her lover back to her. Elizabeth comes to distinguish unthinking prejudice from impartial judgment, and so can love and be loved by Mr Darcy. Jane Austen defines our faults for us, analyses our virtues, and tells us that if we will only control the one with the other, all will yet be well.

That to be good is to be happy is not something particularly evident in any of our experiences of real life, yet how badly we want it, and need it, to be true. Of course we read and re-read Jane Austen.

It is in this sense that the City of Invention is so valuable to us. In this other City, virtue is rewarded, and the bad are punished; and all events are interconnected, and what is more, they rise out of characters and action, not chance. Had you noticed how rarely coincidence occurs in the City of Invention? It is frowned upon here: it upsets the visitors. Coincidence happens in real life all the time. Not here. Cause and effect must rule, or else the readers will prefer reality, with its chaos and coincidence. They will leave the City, in droves.

We want and need to be told how to live. Let me quote from *What is to be Done?*, written by Nicolai Chernyshevsky in 1862. People have been reading it for more than a hundred years. Virago have just re-issued it. *What is to be Done?* is what's called a World Bestseller as is *Emma*. It is a study in self-control and moral development as is *Pride and Prejudice*. It is the story of a girl from a brutal background who grows into a fine young woman, runs a dress factory cooperative in Czarist Russia and becomes a doctor.

She marries twice: the first marriage is sexless, since the sexual act is seen as something rather animal and undignified and standing in the way of true companionship and true love: in the second marriage sex is allowable as an expression of love. Chernyshevsky almost seems to be saying, like St Paul, 'Well, better to marry, I suppose, than to burn.' He offers us an agreeable and stirring and achievable Utopia, if only we would learn to control ourselves and our passions. He does not invoke God, as the Church does, as the interventionary power required to bring general self-control and Heaven here on earth: he sees the strength latent there in both man and woman, if only they will use it.

It is stirring stuff: we should have more of it. He addresses his reader boldly, thus:

> I wager that up to the concluding paragraphs Vera, Kirsanov and Lopukhov (his protagonists) have seemed to the majority of the public to be heroes, individuals of a superior nature, if not ideal persons, if not every person's impossible aim in real life by reason of their very noble conduct. No, my poor friends, you have been wrong in this thought: they are not too high. It is you who are too low. You see now that they simply stand on the surface of the earth: and, if they have seemed to you to be soaring in the clouds, it is because you are in the infernal depths. The light where they stand all men should and can reach. . . . Come up from your caves, my friends, ascend! It is not so difficult. Come to the surface of this earth, where one is so well situated and the road is easy and attractive. Try it: development! development! Observe, think, read those who tell you of the pure enjoyment of life, of the possible goodness and happiness of men.

Chernyshevsky was, if you want a rapid résumé of nineteenth-century Russian thought, a 'man of the 'eighties', who replaced the men of the 'sixties, with more visionary Utopians – Kropotkin the anarchist, Bakunin the philosopher. (They couldn't stand each other.) Chernyshevsky ran off with Bakunin's daughter and was mad, quite mad. He frightened everyone with his glittering eyes. He was arrested for his revolutionary activities when he was thirty-four, tried and sentenced to life imprisonment. He escaped, they say, by converting the entire prison staff to his ideas, to the kind of ecstatic pre-Marxist communism we find in *What is to be Done?*, which he wrote in prison. The staff unlocked the prison gates and set him free. The authorities found him, and sent him to Siberia where the warders were less impressionable and too stupid and vile to be converted to anything, and where he died in 1889. *What is to be Done?* lives on.

Jane Austen's lifestyle (as they call it now) was very different, and her call to moral arms more muted; but it was there. And her books too live on.

Well, of course readers are envious of writers.

With best wishes,
Aunt Fay

Letter to a sister

Canberra, January

My dear Enid,

Thank you for writing to me. Your letter followed me from Cairns, and has caught me here the day before I leave for Heathrow. Of course I am not encouraging your daughter Alice to write a novel. Of course she should concentrate on her studies. I am only trying to help her understand Jane Austen: see my letters as seed flung upon ground badly in need of literary fertilizer.

Do you remember our mother discovering a copy of *The Well of Loneliness* under my pillow and ceremoniously burning it, as indecent and likely to corrupt? Did you ever report that incident to Alice? I doubt it, yet the title is lurking there somewhere in her subconscious: it would almost lead one to become a Lamarckian, and believe in the inheritance of acquired characteristics.

I *am* glad you wrote. It is time we patched up this quarrel. I understand your nervousness that Alice might set fictional pen to paper – you are particularly sensitive on this point and no doubt believe she will start writing about your and Edward's intimate marital relationship for all the world to see, and then Edward will ban her from the house. She won't – any more than I ever did. You are *not* the model for Chloe in *Female Friends*. Too many of my friends claim that role, in any case, for you to be able to do so sensibly. Any woman who waits upon her husband as a servant upon a master – and they are legion – all too easily sees herself as Chloe. But I *made her up*. I promise. It is true that you must set the dough to rise before going to bed so that Edward can have fresh home-baked bread rolls for breakfast, as Chloe did for her Oliver, but because you do that, must no writer ever write about it? Can you *own* it, because you *do* it? The incident is yours, I admit, but the character of Chloe simply is not. *You* would never have a garden full of other people's children, come to live with you because you were the only mother in sight. You choose your friends more carefully. You will never leave Edward, crying 'I can, I can, and I will!' and good for you, because you live the way you live, however strange that may appear to others. You are not Chloe.

Let me try and explain; let me try and give you proof. There is, to me, even as reader, a detectable difference between invented and described characters. Take Miss Bates in Jane Austen's *Emma* – a book I know you have read and loved, though somehow failed to pass the enthusiasm on to little punk-head Alice. I am sure Miss Bates is based upon a real person, 'a woman that one may, that one *must* laugh at,' says Emma – because it is a slightly spiteful portrait and goes on too long: Jane Austen's revenge perhaps for hours of local boredom. Truly, properly invented characters, born out of the imagination, sprung from the head fully formed, as Venus was from Zeus, may appear as wicked, or good, or bizarre or foolish, but the writer takes the attitude of God – he forgives and understands, even while condemning. This is, after all, his own creation. He is in a way responsible.

But when the writer describes and does not invent, he suffers the limitations of his own humanity, and appears spiteful, or bigoted, or not really entitled to comment at all. Miss Bates, I confess, makes me uneasy. I think she lived in the village of Chawton, and I am sure the villagers read *Emma* and nudged each other and said, 'That's her, that's Miss Bates,' and laughed the more at her, and I hope Jane Austen was slightly ashamed, just as Emma eventually was. Except, of course, literacy in the village would have been running at a rate of only some fifteen per cent. Perhaps Jane Austen thought she was safe.

Authors writhe and chafe at the notion that they are parasitical upon spouses, family, friends, colleagues. The charge is so nearly true, yet never quite. People in fiction are conglomerates or abstractions: in personality and in appearance. Fictional characters are simple and understandable – real people are infinitely complex, incomprehensible and even in appearance look one way one day and another the next.

Of course I am worried that you think you are Chloe, and I feel guilty about it, even while loudly declaring my innocence.

But these kind of literary-social personal remarks are better directed at Alice, who has essays to write and needs a phrase here and a thought there, not you, Enid. My love to Edward. If he will forgive me for upsetting you by putting before the general novel-reading public (a *very* small proportion of the population, I do assure him – and Mrs Thatcher *never* reads them) the details of husband/wife bread roll relationships, and accept that my whole purpose in the world is *not* to upset marriages, and will understand that my sending Alice £500 was not in order to denigrate him, or imply that he kept his own daughter in poverty, but simply a matter of paying off my gambling debts in an honourable way, I would love to come to stay. I do miss you, Enid.

Your loving sister,\
Fay

Emma lives!

Singapore, February

My dear Alice,

I am in correspondence with your mother: your father may forgive me: we may even be reunited. Why any of us read novels, life being so novelettish, I cannot today imagine. Next week, jet-lagged and with the prospect of an earnest, hard-working future unalleviated by foreign travel before me, I shall no doubt be knocking pitifully once again on the doors of the City, in flight from boredom, in search of ideas.

In the meantime, I am on the 18th floor of the Marco Polo Stopover hotel, too terrified of the East to leave my room. My terror is not for my body but for my mind. To come to terms with the concept of the group soul, and forget our Western notion of individual life, death and salvation, takes more time than is available to me on this trip. I shall look out of the window and pretend that what I see is a backcloth, and write to you, and have hamburgers for supper, and shut my senses to the ripe, Imperial, murderous efficiency of this new/old place, on the Qantas coach back to beautiful Changi airport, where the fountains play and policemen with machine guns keep them trained upon the crowd, no doubt for the benefit of the likes of me. I carry Currency.

I think you should make yourself acquainted with the writers Jane Austen read: Addison, Johnson, Sheridan, Goldsmith, Richardson, Fielding, Sterne and Fanny Burney.

Too much?

Stick to Fielding. Read *Tom Jones* (if *that's* too much, at least see the film). Jane Austen is said to have censured Fielding as being morally lax. One of the difficulties of being a writer of note is that people believe that you mean what you say, and believe that you go on believing what you say. A change of mind or mood requires a flag or a trumpet. Had Jane Austen known that a light remark of hers about Fielding – possibly uttered to suit the occasion and keep the social wheels running smoothly – was to stand as her one, true, lasting opinion of Fielding through the centuries, she might well have phrased it differently – or, had she wanted to get on with her work, simply given the existing statement marks out of ten for conviction, durability and passionate utterance, and marked all rather low.

I think you should probably read Richardson's *Sir Charles Grandison*, which I believe was one of Jane Austen's favourites. I have not read it. If you will read it, Alice, and let me know what it is like, I will pay you £50. I believe that reading books you do not really want to read, like looking after children you do not really want to look after, should be a very highly-paid occupation indeed. It is an assault to the human spirit. I studied English Literature for a short (a very short) time at university, and was so distressed at having to read a novel by Walter Scott that I paid someone else to do it, in much the same way as I now pay you for reading Richardson. It was not an admirable or ethical act, in the circumstances, and feeling it to be so, I gave up English Literature altogether, and took to Economics and Psychology, departments in which I flourished. I deduce nothing from this, either as to the nature of the reader or the embryo writer, merely that I was a bored and idle student. I hope *you* never do any such thing.

I wonder if you are a politicized young woman? I wonder if you notice that your examinations become more and more difficult to pass as there are fewer and fewer places available in our universities? Or, if you know, perhaps you do not care? You are, I suspect, too privileged, too bright, too pretty, too secure in your opinions to care much what goes on in your society. And, above all, too unread, too little practised in empathy.

Jane Austen wrote her first version of *Pride and Prejudice* (then called *First Impressions*) in 1796. It was a year of famine and shortages. The price of wheat was rocketing. There was large-scale rural unemployment – most workers on the land were temporary employees, and in hard times were left without work. Nearly everyone worked at harvest time – almost nobody at Christmas. If there was no work there were no wages, and if there were no wages there was no food. More children died, inside or outside the womb. The villagers still doffed their caps to the gentry, and especially to the vicar who, leaving his relationship to God out of it, was usually the magistrate, and had almost total power in the community; to sentence for offences, to grant relief, to evict, and so forth. No doubt the vicar's children were well and truly doffed to. What should they notice? They took soup to the poor, and did not wonder at the causes of their poverty. They took comfort, if they did, in the existence of the Speenhamland system – which came into being in the mid-1770s, and which subsidized low wages out of the local rates in cases where the labourer's family income fell below the subsistence level, either because the price of bread was too high or because he had too many children. It was never law, but it was certainly common, and it never worked. The distinction between worker and pauper vanished. Farmers continued to pay below-subsistence rates. The subsistence level itself was whittled away. In 1795 a three-and-a-half gallon loaf did for an adult male, a one-and-a-half for every other member of his family: twenty years later a one gallon loaf per adult male was considered appropriate. That's the way it goes.

The rural population saw its common land vanishing as farmers and landowners claimed it for their own, and enclosed it with hedges, and was powerless to prevent it, and grew hungrier and hungrier.

And Mr Bingley rode by the Bennets' window on his way to Netherfield Park, and Elizabeth was slighted by Darcy, and sister Jane was slighted by Mr Bingley, and then Darcy fell in love with Elizabeth, who rejected his offer of marriage, and Lydia ran off and lived in sin for at least a week with Mr Wickham, and Elizabeth fell in love with Darcy, and Bingley was reunited with Jane, and everyone lived happily ever after, even Mrs Bennet, the only one with the slightest notion of the sheer desperation of the world, whom everyone laughed at throughout.

Nonsense, isn't it!

Millions starving, then and now, I hear you protesting. And Jane Austen! What *are* you going on about? All I can answer is, plaintively, man, and especially woman, does not live by bread alone: he has to have books.

Not that *Pride and Prejudice* would have cheered the lives of the rural poor, for so few of them could read. The Rev. Austen was busy teaching the sons of the gentry Latin; not the sons of the poor to read and write. That way revolution lay – or at any rate uncomfortable demands for higher wages.

Emma Woodhouse befriended Harriet in *Emma* and Harriet was born in rather sorry circumstances and Emma tried to teach her, but I'm afraid in eighteenth-century terms breeding will out – Harriet was a disappointment to Emma. Mr Knightley knew it would be so. The argument then was all from nature, not nurture. In the genes v. environment debate, genes won hands down, even in Jane Austen. Harriet found her natural level with honest Robert Martin, tenant farmer. The gentry, if misbegotten, went down a fairly sharpish peg or so.

So what *are* you going on about? I hear you repeat. Why this reverence for Jane Austen, who was blind (in our terms) to so much? I will tell you. The gentry, then as now, *has* to read in order to comprehend both the wretchedness and ire of the multitude. It is not only ignorance in the illiterate we need to combat, it is insensitivity in the well-to-do. Fiction stretches our sensibilities and our understanding, as mere information never can. Well, you will know this for yourself. A play on television makes ten times the impact as a documentary on the same subject. (I am talking about plays – not series episodes. The play is the controlled fantasy of a single person, and the technology follows where he or she – usually he – leads. The series episode is the product of group thinking, and will hold the mind of the viewer but not his or her – usually her – imagination.)

If society is to advance then those that hath must empathize with those that hath not. I am not offering quite so severe a doctrine as Auden's – 'we must love one another or die' – rather that we must learn to stand in other people's shoes and look out at the world with their eyes, or die. (It is at least a little more attainable to most people, love being in such scarce supply and depending – or so they say – on love of self, which is scarcely within our control.) If the Minister of Education and the Prime Minister read more novels, your exams would not be so difficult to pass, university places having been cut. They would know what if *felt* like to be an unsuccessful student, and they would have mercy.

You can practise the art of empathy very well in *Pride and Prejudice*, and in all the novels of Jane Austen, and it is this daily practice that we all need, or we will never be good at living, as without practice we will never be good at playing the piano.

The writer, oddly enough, holding master classes in empathy, is excused from his or her obligation to observe the distress of society, to record the wider sweeps of social change. More than enough to observe and pass on the minutiae of the dealings between one human being and another: it is up to others to extrapolate from the small to the great, from the microcosm to the greater world. I have heard it offered as a reason (or excuse, I suppose) for the fact that a whole band of writers appears to espouse fascist causes, is because – dealing so intently with the fictional world, needing all their energy for the building of their splendid houses in the City of Invention – they like to be able to relax in the real world, and leave its conduct to the strong and powerful; those who cannot, in fact, be argued with. Discuss, on one side of the paper only.

I have had my Sunset Daiquiri brought to me by Room Service, and also a club sandwich filled with curry. Thus East and West must meet. Room Service – as often happens when ladies of a certain age travel alone – also offered more intimate services, which I refused. Your mother would be proud of me – your father merely conclude that women who travel alone deserve whatever they get. I know a young woman who travelled the world fomenting revolution and when she got home to her parents' house in leafy Muswell Hill complained tearfully of having been raped by five policemen on the Afghanistan border, and was met by 'well, what do you expect?' She took great exception to this, but I think I am on her parents' side. Nothing is for nothing. The world is very real, and not made up of an insubstantial web of rights and wrongs, and ins and outs, as we like to think in our leafy, decent suburbs, and it is no use being astonished – as journalists often are – if you join a war and are shot by real and not theoretical bullets, often by your own side. Because one cause is bad does not make the opposing cause good. It is a hard lesson, lately learned.

I have put the chain on my door and re-read your letter. You complain about *Emma*. You say you have read the first third. I will admit there is a middle section of *Emma* which drags, rather.

Let me give you a quick run-down of the plot – the peg upon which Jane Austen hangs her novels. Plots, I assure you, are nothing but pegs. They stand in a row in the writer's mind. You can use one or another for your purposes, it makes some difference, but not much, which one it is. The plot of *Emma* is not quite so flimsy as that of *Pride and Prejudice*: it can support altogether more character, and more observation, and more meaning: and more boredom on the part of the grudging and hasty reader – in whose ranks I still include you.

If you want *real* enthusiasm, read Ronald Blythe's introduction to the novels in the Penguin series. '*Emma* is the climax of Jane Austen's genius and the Parthenon of fiction', it begins. They won't allow *you* to be so dramatic and positive in your essays on the book: they will feel you are throwing words around like weapons, to parry attack: but that is because they, like me, are suspicious of your youth, and how easily ignorance and enthusiasm blend, like eggs into choux pastry, making the whole, when baked, rise and puff and grow light: empty, mere shells, requiring to be filled.

Emma opens with a paragraph which sends shivers of pleasure down my spine: it glitters with sheer competence: with the animation of the writer who has discovered power: who is at ease in the pathways of the City of Invention. Here is Emma, exciting envy in the heart of the reader and also, one suspects, the writer – and now, she declares, Emma will be undone; and I, the writer, and you, the reader, will share in this experience:

> Emma Woodhouse, handsome, clever and rich, with a comfortable home and happy disposition, seemed to unite some of the best blessings of existence: and had lived nearly twenty-one years in the world with very little to distress or vex her . . .

It's the word 'seemed', fourteen in, which sets the whole book up. It will take four hundred pages to resolve. You have five variations there – handsome, clever, rich, comfortable home, happy disposition – five to the power of five, which you can relate in various combinations of the 'blessings of existence'.

It is so simple, you see, and so wonderfully full of promise, which bypasses the conscious mind of the reader, gets us instantly into the City of Invention, and off we go.

I frequently find myself saying to unpublished and resentful writers who do not understand the reason for their rejection, 'but you must think of your *readers*', and they think I am telling them to write for a market, but I am not. I am trying to explain that writing must be in some way a shared experience between reader and writer: the House of Imagination built with doors for guests to enter in, and pegs for their coats, and windows for them to look out of: it is no use being a recluse. You will die of hypothermia and malnutrition if you live alone in your house, however beautifully constructed it is. It must be a welcoming place, or exciting, if dangerous, or educative, if unpleasant, or intensely pleasurable.

Emma lives with her (to me, but not Emma) irritating, difficult, hypochondriacal father, Mr Woodhouse, in the village of Hartfield. Her mother died in her infancy: she has a married sister, Isabella. She has £30,000 of her own. She was brought up by a governess, who presently marries, thanks to Emma's matchmaking, and leaves Emma lonely. She is conceited. There is a fairly obvious suitor in the village, a Mr Knightley; but Emma sees him in the role of friend, not lover. (Lover in the old sense of suitor, Alice. Fornication was simply not in the minds of decent and self-controlled people, for reasons I have already gone into.) Another possible lover is approaching over the horizon – a Frank Churchill – brought up, like her own brother, Edward, in rather grander circumstances than the ones into which he was born. Emma has befriended Harriet Smith; Harriet Smith is a beautiful but misbegotten girl. 'The misfortune of your birth ought to make you particularly careful of your associates,' Emma warns her. Illegitimate! Harriet is on the verge of marrying Robert Martin, farmer, but Emma, believing Harriet could do better in the marriage stakes, turns the foolish girl against poor Mr Martin. Mr Knightley reproaches her for this. Emma means Harriet to marry Mr Elton, the handsome curate, and mistakes his courtesy to Harriet for passion. Mr Knightley reproaches her. Jane Fairfax appears as a foil to Emma – more talented, more clever, and more serious than her, and doomed to be misunderstood, and ever so slightly disliked. (I wonder sometimes if Jane Fairfax is not more of a self-portrait of Jane Austen than Elizabeth Bennet – the bright, lovable, wayward heroine of *Pride and Prejudice*, as is so often supposed.) Emma is unkind to Miss Bates. Mr Knightley reproaches her. Mr Elton takes a detestable wife. In and out the relationships intertwine.

Ronald Blythe, in his loyalty, describes the ins and outs as a 'detective story', and you would do better to believe him than me if you want to pass your exams. But it was written in 1814–15. I believe that Jane Austen, from the internal evidence of *Emma*, was at that time driven to distraction by her mother and Cassandra, and to boredom by the manner of her life, and not quite having the courage to go to the kind of parties where Madame de Staël would appear, and developing a fatal illness, and humiliated by living in a corner house in the village by courtesy of her brother, who lived up in the big house, when the Prince Regent had a set of her books in each of his houses. I think she wrote on, gritting her teeth, wrapping her misery into herself, taking refuge in the world of invention, instead of going there with a clear mind and heart, travelling freely in and out, unable quite to get the coat properly off the peg. She kept tugging and it wouldn't come; and that is why you have no trouble with the first third of the book and then stopped reading. She was having trouble too.

She did get it off the hook. Harriet develops aspirations to Mr Knightley which shocks Emma into realizing her own love for him. Harriet's origins are discovered to be even lower than at first thought, so she can be safely married to Robert Martin. The odious Mr Woodhouse is talked into liking the idea of Mr Knightley and Emma marrying. The intimacy between Emma and Harriet changes into a calmer sort of goodwill. Well, it would have to, wouldn't it, if Emma is going to be Mrs Knightley. Some have doubted that the marriage of Emma to Mr Knightley is indeed a happy ending, but I am content to let Jane Austen know her own characters best.

We return, very much, in all this, to the 'breeding must out' preoccupation of the times. Emma befriends Harriet, who was born in such sorry circumstances, and tries to teach and improve her, whilst taking pleasure in her simple gaiety (even then, it seems, the gentry looked a little askance at their own refinement, envying the common herd their general energy and lack of inhibition – as our modern-day cultural spokesman will love to go to football matches, and middle-class young ape the language of the streets, and music critics attempt to take the Beatles seriously, and in general invent art forms which require an untutored imagination rather than a dangerously desiccated expertise) – but Harriet was in the end a disappointment to Emma. Mr Knightley, who knew everything, knew it would be so.

Harriet may have been well born (there were funds for her education, so presumably at least one of her parents had money) but she was not virtuously born; she had better make do with a yeoman farmer for a husband. Seven out of ten for genes, take away three for unfortunate beginnings, add one for a good sound education, another two for prettiness and charm, and take away two for a general lack of soundness and you end up with five out of ten – the same marks as Robert Martin, yeoman farmer, began and ended with; it was therefore a good match. The delight of *Emma* – which I trust by now you have taken up again – is in the violent seesawing of marks out of ten, especially in Harriet's case, which the author awards. Emma herself hovers between seven and eight, losing marks for folly and wilfulness, gaining them for being good to her dreadful father, Mr Woodhouse, losing them (and quite right too) for being so obnoxious to Miss Bates, gaining them again for putting up with grief without making a fuss (unlike Harriet) – and finally making it through to nine out of ten, and thus being allowed to marry Mr Knightley – a steady nine out of ten throughout. And he would have had a ten out of ten, like Mr Darcy, had he been nobly born and about to be a Marquis any minute.

(It is observable in Jane Austen's novels that it is the women who have moral struggles, rather than the men. This may, of course, be a reflection of life. It is because I make this sort of remark that your father will not have me in the house – that and the matter of the bread rolls, of course.)

Jane Austen likes to see the division between nobility and gentry broken down – or perhaps she merely wishes to ennoble the rather dreadful habit the nobility had, of using the gentry as their breeding ground – choosing suitable mothers for their children as they chose mates for their farm animals – liking to 'breed out' in order to achieve healthy stock. They weren't daft. Later, the English nobility were to use the *nouveau riche* American girls for similar purpose – and they, of course, often brought money with them. Elizabeth Bennet brought neither land nor money to Darcy – but she brought intelligence, vigour and honesty. Her vulgar mother, her dreadful sister Lydia, just had, in the end, to be put up with.

(Or, as Winston Churchill would say – himself the son of a love-and-money match between an English Lord and an American heiress – 'up with which in the end everyone would have to put'. It is a truism – at least to my generation – that Churchill sent back for re-writing memoranda containing sentences which ended with prepositions. Even with Hitler battering at the gates, it seemed important. Civilization v. barbarity.)

In general, in the novels of the times, if working girls – governesses, dairy maids and so forth – won the love of gentlemen, some switching at birth is bound to have occurred. Until very recently, the switching of babies, the sending away of rightful heirs and so forth, has been the stock-in-trade of fiction – and not only an attractive idea in the personal sense – which of us, when young, did not stare at our parents and think 'surely, *surely* this can't be them!' – but in the political sense, as a phenomenon, both echoing and leading the groping forward of society, through the fog of custom and prejudice, through to the light at the end of the tunnel, when all men could be reckoned to be born equal. It is out of fashion, now that we are all (more or less) socially mobile.

It is time for me to leave this hotel and return to the care of Quant- Qua- Qantas. (I have had to write that three times before I can manage a 'Q' without a following 'u'.)

I think I have been too scathing about your attempts to write a novel. By all means, try.

Your loving aunt,
Fay

'Oh! It's only a novel!'

London, February

My dear Alice,

It is alarming to be back in this real city, having stayed for so long in what seems, in retrospect, a picture postcard. Australians live on the surface of their vast land, and round its rim: the centre, unimaginably beautiful, is left empty. I am reminded of a human brain, excited activity around its periphery, the slow, blank, powerful unconscious within. Inner space. It is the country of the future, I swear. Little by little that centre will be drawn into consciousness: memories will surface, and something new and immensely wise will be born. In the meantime the land is like some powerful zonked-out god, lying splayed on its back, zapped by the past, stirring the Pacific with an idle toe, suffering from a temporary amnesia. Just you wait till it wakes: be there if you possibly can, citizen of no mean city. Do you know that reference? 'I am a citizen of no mean city'? St Paul?

In 1797 the Reverend Austen wrote to the London publisher Cadell, saying he was in possession of a novel about the length of Burney's *Evelina*, which he would forward if Cadell was interested. Cadell wrote back declining the offer, thus calling down upon himself hoots of derision from an unfeeling future. The novel was *Pride and Prejudice*. Now I don't blame Cadell at all. The novel must have sounded singularly ordinary. Poor girl gets rich man in unbelievable circumstances: the setting rather mundane. The nearest thing to High Life, a guided tour by a housekeeper around a stately home. . . . Popular novels of the time fell easily into one of two categories – novels of Sentiment and novels of Terror. *Pride and Prejudice* was clearly one of the former, but lacked the death scenes which were so popular. Nobody even swooned. Jane caught a bad cold, but that hardly counted.

And in any case, novels of Terror, the same gothic novels that we have, early versions of our bodice-rippers, sold better.

Now, you must remember, Alice, that at the time to *read* novels was a highly suspect activity. The human appetite for fiction, not unlike the human appetite for sex, though in a milder degree, was seen as somehow sleazy. (How much more disconcerting to have someone in the family who actually *wrote* them.) It had become quite the fashionable thing for women of good education, lively mind and no occupation to turn their hand to the task, but they were expected to take great care not to offend, to set a good moral tone, in general to encourage the reader towards virtue and good behaviour. Most certainly the Reverend Austen would not have sent *Lady Susan* to Mr Cadell – the tale of a wicked woman, who although punished by being obliged to marry the horrible suitor she had planned as her daughter's husband, seemed, in the meantime, to enjoy her wicked ways, and who had a *Good Time*. Had Jane Austen been born to a different, wilder, freer background, had she kept company with Shelley and his wife Mary of Frankenstein fame, Byron and his sister Augusta, of incest fame, and Leigh Hunt, of grasshopper fame – but such suppositions are as much nonsense as wishing one had been born to different parents. If one had, one would not exist.

Anyway, *Pride and Prejudice*, under its original title *First Impressions* was not accepted by Mr Cadell.

If you persist with your novel, Alice, you will find it difficult to finish. Because if you finish it you will then have the problem of whether or not you actually *want* it published. The worry may be conscious, or unconscious, but it will be there. You will go on holiday, break an arm, finish with a boyfriend, or start another affair; quarrel with your parents, burn down your flat – anything, to put off the actual finishing of the work. You may very well not even understand what you are doing.

'But I couldn't have *wanted* to break my arm,' you'll say.

'Your right arm,' I'll say, 'your writing arm. Funny it wasn't your left.'

And it will be unfair but there'll be a truth in it. You are building your house in the City of Invention: the responsibility terrifies you. Presently you will have to throw open the doors – and supposing no one wants to come in? Or even worse, supposing they do? Won't life change? Won't you have to put aside the griefs and complaints that sustain you, and embark on a whole new set? Oh yes, indeed. Success is a dreadful thing.

Especially, I will add, *pace* your father, especially for a woman. For if you can look after yourself, who will look after you? 'Success kicks away the stool of masochism, on which female existence so often depends, and leaves you hanging, gasping.' Discuss.

And there's another factor, too. Sir Thomas More put it rather elegantly in 1515, in his *Utopia*, translated with equal elegance in 1965 by Paul Turner:

> To tell you the truth, though, I still haven't made up my mind whether I shall publish it at all. Tastes differ so widely, and some people are so humourless, so uncharitable, and so absurdly wrong-headed, that one would probably do far better to relax and enjoy life than worry oneself to death trying to instruct or entertain a public which will only despise one's efforts, or at least feel no gratitude for them. Most readers know nothing about literature – many regard it with contempt. Lowbrows find everything heavy going that isn't completely low-brow. Highbrows reject everything as vulgar that isn't a mass of archaisms. Some only like the classics, others only their own works. Some are so grimly serious that they disapprove of all humour, others so half-witted that they can't stand wit. Some are so literal-minded that the slightest hint of irony affects them as water affects a sufferer from hydrophobia. Others come to different conclusions every time they stand up or sit down. Then there's the alcoholic school of critics, who sit in public houses, pronouncing *ex cathedra* verdicts of condemnation, just as they think fit. They seize upon your publications, as a wrestler seizes upon his opponent's hair, and use them to drag you down, while they themselves remain quite invulnerable, because their barren pates are completely bald – so there's nothing for you to get hold of.
>
> Besides, some readers are so ungrateful that, even if they enjoy a book immensely, they don't feel any affection for the author. They're like rude guests who after a splendid dinner-party go home stuffed with food, without saying a word of thanks to their host. So much for the wisdom of preparing a feast of reason at one's own expense for a public with such fastidious and unpredictable tastes, and with such a profound sense of gratitude!

Nothing changes for the writer. The centuries revolve around him-her with their changing *mores*, their ever-improving methods of communication – but the activity is timeless, as is the reception of that activity.

And how, if you write novels, are you going to live with your friends and neighbours, who are bound to see themselves therein? They will devour your books simply to do so. They will still confide in you, but they will draw back, saying, 'I suppose you're going to put all this into your next', and that's hurtful. The writer is not parasitical in the way that they suppose. Everything is fed in, it is true, to that unstoppable inner computer: there is no helping that, but it is the stuff, not the substance, of what is regurgitated; there is something besides, so oddly impersonal about it all. As if the computer merely used the writer as its eyes and ears: as if it were that fate took a hand, made this particular person act in a certain way, only for the recording. Fiction first, life after. It is an intolerable thought.

As if it were decreed that your mother Enid should put bread rolls to rise every night for your father Edward's breakfast, in order that a certain paragraph in a certain novel should be written.

As if the City of Invention, little by little, using a chapter here, a paragraph there, is waking from its slumber and will eventually be more real than life itself, and we its servants, its outrunners.

By the time you have finished your novel you will know what I mean.

With love,
Fay

'I never read much'

Somerset, March

My dear Alice,

How can I possibly tell you how to run your life? I am a novelist and your aunt, not a seer. I suppose I could offer a few general rules. For example:

1. Love your mother if you possibly can, since she is the source of your life.
2. Love men if you possibly can, since they are the source of your gratification.
3. Reform yourself, as well as the world.
4. Agree with your accusers, loudly and clearly. They will shut up sooner.
5. Worry less about what other people think of you, and more about what you think of them.

I shall leave 6, 7, 8, 9 and 10 blank, for you to fill in yourself. Revise them every New Year's Day. The real Secret of Life lies in Constant Rule Revision.

I can offer, more sensibly, a few general rules about writing:

(a) Show your work to no one, not to friend, nor spouse, nor anyone. They know no better than you, but will have to say something. The publisher or producer, eventually, will say yes or no, which are the only words you need to hear.

You won't observe this rule: so:

(b) What others say are your faults, your weaknesses, may if carried to extremes be your virtues, your strengths. *I* don't like too many adjectives or adverbs – I say if a noun or a verb is worth describing, do it properly, take a sentence to do it. There's no hurry. Don't say 'the quick brown fox jumped over the lazy dog'. Say, 'it was at this moment that the fox jumped over the dog. The fox was brown as the hazelnuts in the tree hedgerows, and quick as the small stream that ran beside, and the dog too lazy to so much as turn his head.' Or something. Writing is more than just the making of a series of comprehensible statements: it is the gathering in of connotations; the harvesting of them, like blackberries in a good season, ripe and heavy, snatched from among the thorns of logic.

Having thus discouraged the apprentice writer from over-use of adjectives, I turn at once to Iris Murdoch and find she will use eighteen of them in a row. It works. What is weakness in small quantities, is style in overdose. So be wary of anyone who tries to teach you to write. Do it yourself. Stand alone. You will never be better than your own judgment, and you will never be satisfied with what you do. Ambition will, and should, always outstrip achievement.

(c), (d), (e) and (f) you can fill in for yourself.

You tell me the plot of your novel in a nutshell. It sounds perfectly dreadful. But then so does *Pride and Prejudice* in a nutshell. (I know! Witches used to go to sea in nutshells? Wrong again! Eggshells, a friend says. That's why children turn their eaten boiled eggs over and smash the shells. To thwart the witches. And I'd thought it was just their general tendency to leave me to clear up the detail of their self-expression. But I broke my eggshells as a child: so did your mother: I expect you do too. It is the kind of thing that gets handed on, like life expectancy, rolling acres, and cold sores.)

I will tell you that the main fault of young writers is their habit of writing about the love lives of themselves and their friends, since this is so boring to the truly adult reader – inasmuch as what strikes the young as exciting and amazing is to the more experienced observer trite beyond belief, and boring too, and I will suggest that you wait until you have met an actual trouble or two, and know yourself a little better, and lose your good opinion of yourself, and get on with your studies, as your mother and father are so anxious that you should and then events will prove me wrong and you right. It is the kind of thing that happens.

I am wrong about things two times out of five. My general impression about other people is that they are wrong two-and-a-half times out of five. Can this be success? I know a brain surgeon. She plunges about with lasers in the brains of people who will die if she does nothing. Sometimes she cures them totally, sometimes she kills them quickly, sometimes she reduces them to long-lasting vegetables. But someone has to do something. And her vegetation rate, as it's called, is two out of ten and not three out of ten, as it is with her colleagues, and her death rate the same, so she is considered The Best. And is. And people queue up – if people in comas can be said to queue up – for her services.

Your novel is about a young girl studying English Literature who falls in love with her professor, who is married to someone unlovable, and how her boyfriend reacts, which is not as expected. (It's how *I* expect, who have some knowledge of human depravity.) He has an affair with Unlovable. It is all, obviously, autobiographical. My advice to you is, consider the nature of Unlovable. You may be wrong about her.

May I also suggest that your falling in love is an example of those diversionary tactics which afflict the writer – (I have already described them) – because in your earlier account of this novel it concerned a young girl studying English Literature who falls in love with a fellow student (male) and so escapes incipient lesbianism. By changing your allegiance to the professor you have altered the course of your novel – or should, unless you want it to be merely episodic – and delayed its finishing.

Why not fall out of love with the professor and go back to your first draft? But I'm afraid you won't. I'm afraid you'll then need a third draft about a young girl falling *out* of love with a married professor – and so on and so on. And will boyfriend then come back to you? He may not, you see. *You* know he's part of your fiction, but he, rightly or wrongly, believes he's living in a real world.

There's no end to it if you go on like this, nor, I fear, of the novel. Novels are not meant to be diaries, you know.

Let me now speak to you seriously about *Northanger Abbey*.

Let me take you into my confidence. Having written the previous sentence I stretched out my hand for *Northanger Abbey* and found it wasn't there. I had left my copy somewhere, in Abu Dhabi, or New York or Colchester, how am I to know? Whereupon I wept, reproached, and disrupted the entire household and became obsessed with the notion that I had not enough bookcases. Writing is all sacrifice, you see, especially on the part of the writer's nearest and dearest. Do not think issuing advice and offering instruction is easy. It makes the body tremble with the notion of one's audacity.

I would rather write a short story than a letter to you any day,
Alice. People could only complain I was boring: they couldn't say I
was wrong, or (at least so much as they did) that I was guilty of
presumption, as you can. You *ask*, but you do not really want me to
answer, I suspect, and on present evidence I am certainly not qualified to do so. Me? Offer advice?

I am much calmer now. I feel guilty, as Frank Churchill was in
Emma's eyes, for 'having let myself get altogether away', and when
I had finished blaming everyone else, blamed you. Then I drove
seven miles to the Bayley Hill Bookshop in Castle Carey, and
bought a new copy of *Northanger Abbey*, and seven miles back, and
on the car radio listened to John Tydeman's admirable dramatiza-
tion of *Emma*, wonderfully produced (in radio they call directors
producers) by Richard Imeson, and almost changed my mind about
the tediousness of several of its chapters, and rejoiced again at the
picnic at Box Hill, where everyone went to be happy and no one
was: it was far too hot; and Mrs Elton bullied Jane Fairfax, and
Emma was so dreadfully unkind to Miss Bates. Emma let her
tongue run away from her; she preferred for an instance the satisfaction of an irritated, witty remark to the satisfaction of being
good and kind; allowed a brusque pattern of words to interrupt the
delicate intertwining of human response, and thus earned Mr
Knightley's reproaches and her own remorse. And such a little
thing! Frank Churchill says everyone must say three boring things.
Miss Bates, desirous of compliment, offers to do it. Emma says, in
effect, but we have a difficulty here. What, only three! Miss Bates,
when do you ever stop?, and Miss Bates, stricken and publicly
humiliated says, I must learn to hold my tongue.

All our lives, on whatever scale they are lived, however studded
with events, sexual obsession, divorce, cancer, the making and
breaking of fortunes, public recognition or approbation, reduce
themselves at times, like some rich sauce over a low flame, to these
little, powerful, painful simmerings, where small events loom im-
passively large. A picnic on Box Hill on a summer's day, when
everything goes wrong; to be remembered, in real life in the future,
after a fashion, but never quite, as it were, head-on. The mind slips
away, hastily gets round, somehow, like a car going into rapid
reverse, grating its gears, when it encounters these small, scraping

memories, which do not count as Major Life Events (to use the terminology of the times), do not merit Working Through, but are simply there, and one wishes they weren't. Social lapses; most embarrassing moments; carcinogenic rubbings in the mind. Long years with a psychoanalyst will smooth them over, listening to *Emma* on the radio will do pretty well, sharing this fictional understanding, not just with *Emma*'s writer, but with all her readers as well. A package tour to the City of Invention!

Alice, does it not seem to you most extraordinary: the amazing phenomenon of shared fantasy. I can never get used to it. I suppose half a million people listened to *Emma* this afternoon; of those a few hundred thousand would already know the book; a few thousand, with me, would be willing and wishing Emma *not* to say what she did say, while knowing that indeed she would say it:

> Miss Bates: 'I shall be sure to say three dull things as soon as ever I open my mouth, shan't I?' (looking round with the most good-humoured dependence on everybody's assent). 'Do not you all think I shall?'
> Emma could not resist.
> Emma: 'Ah! ma'am, but there may be a difficulty. Pardon me, but you will be limited as to number – only three at once!'

Alice, Emma lives!

Or let me put it another way, if that makes you shuffle and feel uneasy. (There are more ways of killing a cat, and making a Jane Austen convert, than you would suppose.) All over the country irons were held in suspension, and car exhaust bandages held motionless and lady gardeners stayed their gardening gloves, and cars slowed, as Emma spoke, as that other world intruded into this. It does more and more, you know. We join each other in shared fantasies, it is our way of crossing barriers, when our rulers won't let us. E.T. and his like is our real communication. Hand in hand the human race abandons the shoddy, imperfect structures of reality, and surges over to the City of Invention.

(I suppose to you it appears quite ordinary: for you the world has always trembled on the verge of the fictional supra-reality: *Dr Who* flows in your bloodstream. It still, as a phenomenon, leaves me feeling breathless.)

O.K. Back to *Northanger Abbey*. In my edition (Oxford World's Classics) I observe that the editor (John Davie) has, according to his publishers, researched on authors as diverse as Jane Austen and Browning. It is this kind of remark that makes me feel really inadequate as aunt, semi-literary tutor, and moral adviser. Is not Browning a poet? Is not Jane Austen a novelist? Are they then both to be grouped as authors? Can comparison then be made, or as in this case, anti-comparisons? To say 'as diverse as Jane Austen and Jorge-Luis Borges' would make more sense. Jane Austen and Browning simply doesn't. Unless there is something I *don't know*, and Browning wrote novels as well as poetry. (Did he? Did he? At moments like these I wish I had persisted with Eng. Lit. I am sure it is the kind of thing everyone else knows, but me.) And who am I to find fault with the editors of the Oxford University Press?

I raise this point, Alice, in the hope that you will not begin the suspension of your disbelief until you have actually got to the text of whatever you are reading; the phrase 'as diverse as Jane Austen and Browning', if you allow it to penetrate your young and all too penetrable mind, will muddle and confuse your mental filing system. You will forever be pulling things out of the wrong places. You must always be more on your guard, when reading non-fiction, as I like to rather affectedly and disparagingly call it, than fiction.

And do remember, a letter counts as non-fiction. Careful, Alice. Use what I say as a sack of rather dusty brown rice, from which you will take cupfuls, at intervals, and concoct delicious and nourishing dishes. (You mention in your letter that you are a vegetarian. Your Marxist Professor (married) of Economics is a vegetarian too. That surprises me. Marxists are usually meat-eaters. It is the softer, more liberal left which feels tender about lately living things.) What I say, remember, is not the dish itself, merely a rather lulling ingredient, to be used at your discretion. Use *your* judgment, Alice, not mine.

Personally, I don't like brown rice at all. I find it difficult to swallow. Sticks in the gullet. Go by instinct, Alice, too. Rely on what you *feel* about books, while remembering it is disgraceful to toss your head and say, 'I know what I like', if only because by the time you've aligned these two rather different activities, knowing and liking, both may somehow have slipped away. You've confined each within the bounds of the other: Siamese twins, back to back, trapped, lashing out at the world, most destructively.

Travel hopefully, as a reader. Retain your trust, as long as you possibly can. My bathroom contains seven half-finished thrillers. I push myself beyond endurance, in the face of bad writing (by this I mean, I think, imprecision in writing, combined with a paucity of thought and feeling, but more of this later), hoping to be held and entranced. And what pleasure there is when, rarely, a good, intelligent, well-worked thriller turns up – I tell you, there shall be more rejoicing in the bathroom over one writer that is lost, and found again. . . .

Alice, I do have to stop now. *Northanger Abbey* will have to wait 'til the next letter. I shall be serious and responsible, I promise. The novel was written in 1798, or thereabouts, when Jane Austen was in her early twenties, was sent to a publisher who bought it but kept it for ten years and didn't publish it. I have some sympathy with him. It isn't nice to be mocked.

In 1798 Napoleon invaded Europe and Jane's wild cousin (well, she married a foreigner, a Frenchman and a royalist, and wore flashy gowns) had fled to England, home and safety with her baby son, and Jane's aunt (her mother's brother's wife) was accused of shoplifting – the penalty if she was found guilty was hanging at worst and transportation at best – and God knows what dreadful things were happening in Ireland, and Jane Austen wrote *Northanger Abbey*, in which the worst thing that happened was that Catherine was sent home in sudden disgrace by her boyfriend's father, General Tilney.

All love,
Aunt Fay

P.S. Mrs Leigh Perrot was acquitted, but only after she had spent many months in jail awaiting trial. She could have bought the shopkeeper off, as he expected, but Mr Leigh Perrot said, 'No, I will never submit to blackmail of this kind!' This story is usually told as demonstrating how noble, likable and admirable a man Mr Leigh Perrot was. But I see it as just more proof of the general premise, that when a man has a principle, a woman pays for it. *He* believes in honour: *she* stays in prison.

'Are you sure they are all horrid?'

London, April

My dear Alice,

I am going to tell you a story you won't believe. A couple of years ago I was being taken home from a party in an art dealer's car, and there beside me on the seat was a packet wrapped in brown paper. I put my hand on it and found that it was warm. Books and papers, similarly placed, were cool enough. I remarked upon it to the art dealer, and he said, 'Well, of course. It's a Lowry. It's a hot property.' I took my hand away rather rapidly. He unwrapped it later and showed it to me. I am not a profound admirer of Lowry's work. I think it is pleasant enough, and leave reverence for those who know more than me. Your mother, for example. (When the qualities were shared out between her and me – as qualities are, among siblings; between them they add up to quite a decent person – she got a visual sense, I got a response to language.) So it was not me endowing the parcel – however telepathically – with a warm importance. I could only imagine it was the intensity of other people's regard, hotting up a mere painting into an actual art object. Lowry had just died; his was the name on many lips, his work a vision in the forefront of many minds, in the strange cultural shadow world where we dwell.

Now, inasmuch as those engaged in particle physics will assure us that a particle alters by virtue of being observed, so we can never really know what anything is like, because the knowledge interferes with what we wish to know, it doesn't surprise me that a painting, so imbued with the force of attention, changes its nature. Heats up. Hot property!

I told you you wouldn't believe me.

But I have had more than one literary critic, adjudicator, panel member, and not all that drunk either, raise his bowed head and say, 'Don't tell anyone. I know it's *mad*. But you begin to know, when you pick up a MS, before you open it, whether it's any good or not. Just something about the *feel*.'

And then, having confided this absurdity, they fall back into their stupor, the paralysis of the over-literate. Enforced judgment thins the blood, in the end. They're the first to agree: they are the slaves to the Muse, not honest yeomen. She uses them and abuses them, sends them chasing off on thankless errands, yet they love her. And it is a noble calling; it is their judgment, after all, that sends the writer or painter off on the strange leaping, bounding, crag-to-crag journey to the summit of their discipline. Hot property!

Desperate would-be writers sometimes send off to those theatrical managements who have rejected their work obscure plays by famous people. When these too are rejected they turn round and say, 'See. We are at the mercy of incompetent and prejudiced judgment! We always knew it. That was a Chekhov play (or whatever) that was!'

But it seems to me that the renown of the writer rubs off on the work itself. That a play written by Ibsen and claimed by Ibsen, is a different and better play than one written by Ibsen and claimed by Anon. The former contains the concentrated magic of the attention of millions; a consensus that here is something, really something; you don't have to join in (like me with Lowry, or rather, *not* with Lowry), but you will know it's there. The latter is merely words upon the page, interpreted by the theatrical profession; it will gain a nod and a snore and an absence, if Anon is lucky, of protest. No more.

How difficult, then, you may say, for the writer to *begin*. Ah yes. We all know that. At which the critics suddenly snap their heads aloft and fix you with a beady and really quite energetic stare and say, 'But that's what we're for. If it wasn't for us, properties would never be hot'.

Northanger Abbey, 1798. A hot property eventually.

Northanger Abbey is a lovely romp. It mocks the kind of novel the publisher Crosby published – the gothic romance, and I am not surprised, having bought it – because how could you *not* buy so spirited, wilful and charming a tale – he felt no need to publish it. He just hung on to it, baffled.

Catherine:

had reached the age of seventeen, without having seen one amiable youth who could call forth her sensibility; without having inspired one real passion, and without having excited even any admiration but what was very moderate and very transient. This was strange indeed! But strange things may be generally accounted for if their cause be fairly searched out. There was not one lord in the neighbourhood; no – not even a baronet. There was not one family among their acquaintance who had reared and supported a boy accidentally found at their door – not one young man whose origin was unknown. Her father had no ward, and the squire of the parish no children.

But when a young lady is to be a heroine, the perverseness of forty surrounding families cannot prevent her. Something must and will happen to throw a hero her way.

It is interesting, is it not, that in her later novels Jane Austen took seriously what in her youth she could not. The stuff of her own later fiction – love at first sight (Jane and Bingley), lords in the neighbourhood (Darcy), wards (Fanny Price and Emma in *The Watsons*), young persons of unknown origin (Harriet Smith) she here derides – well, not quite derides, that is too strong a word, but pokes and prods with a delightedly aware finger. I think it is this ripple of merriment, this underground hilarity, which she has lost by the time she gets to the more plaintive *Mansfield Park* and the more sombre *Persuasion*, that so endeared her to future generations. It may not have shown in her own character; it is, as I like to say to audiences – and I've had my share of them lately, Alice – a literary truth and not a home truth.

How, audiences say to me, can you be married and have sons and still be so horrible about men? And I reply, (a) 'I am not horrible to and about men, I merely report them as I see them. I neither condone nor reproach, I merely report. It's just that men are so accustomed to being flattered in books by women that simple honesty comes as a shock and they register it as biased and unfair' – and if they don't let me get away with that I retreat to, (b) 'This is a literary truth, not a home truth. The writer is not the person, yet both natures are true.'

I think it is perfectly possible that Jane Austen the writer was very different from Jane Austen the person.

I also think, concurrently, that the reason no one married her was the same reason Crosby didn't publish *Northanger Abbey*. It was all just too much. Something truly frightening rumbled there beneath the bubbling mirth: something capable of taking the world by its heels, and shaking it – as a mother takes a choking baby –

shaking out great muddy gobbets of barbarity and incomprehension and cruelty, and setting it on its feet again, altogether better and improved.

She knew too much, you see, for her own good.

> The advantages of natural folly in a beautiful girl have been already set forth by the capital pen of a sister author – and to her treatment of the subject I will only add in justice to men, that though to the larger and more trifling part of the sex, imbecility in females is a great enhancement of their personal charms, there is a portion of them too reasonable and too informed themselves to desire any thing more in women than ignorance.

Can you imagine it?

'And will you dance, Miss Austen, will you dance? You pretty, giddy little thing, with your trim small body and your clear complexion, and your pretty face, perhaps rather too full in the cheeks for perfect beauty – will you dance?' No!

Catherine and Isabella (her friend) shut themselves up, in defiance of wet and dirt, to read novels together:

> Yes, novels; – for I will not adopt that ungenerous and impolitic custom so common with novel writers, of degrading by their contemptuous censure the very performances to the number of which they are themselves adding – joining with their greatest enemies in bestowing the harshest epithets on such works, and scarcely ever permitting them to be read by their own heroine, who, if she accidentally take up a novel, is sure to turn over its insipid pages with disgust. Alas! if the heroine of one novel be not patronized by the heroine of another, from whom can she expect protection and regard? I cannot approve of it. Let us leave it to the Reviewers to abuse such effusions of fancy at their leisure, and over every new novel to talk in threadbare strains of the trash with which the press now groans. Let us not desert one another; we are an injured body. Although our productions have afforded more extensive and unaffected pleasure than those of any other literary corporation in the world, no species of composition has been so much decried. From pride, ignorance, or fashion, our foes are almost as many as our readers. And while the abilities of the nine-hundredth abridger of the History of England, or of the man who collects and publishes in a volume some dozen lines of Milton, Pope and Prior, with a paper from the Spectator, and a chapter from Sterne, are eulogized by a thousand pens – there seems almost a general wish of decrying the capacity and undervaluing the labour of the novelist, and of slighting the performances which have

only genius, wit, and taste to recommend them. 'I am no novel reader – I seldom look into novels – Do not imagine that *I* often read novels – It is really very well for a novel.' – Such is the common cant – 'And what are you reading, Miss –?' 'Oh! it is only a novel!' replies the young lady; while she lays down her book with affected indifference, or momentary shame. – 'It is only Cecilia, or Camilla, or Belinda;' or, in short, only some work in which the greatest powers of the mind are displayed, in which the most thorough knowledge of human nature, the happiest delineation of its varieties, the liveliest effusions of wit and humour are conveyed to the world in the best chosen language. Now, had the same young lady been engaged with a volume of the *Spectator*, instead of such a work, how proudly would she have produced the book, and told its name; though the chances must be against her being occupied by any part of that voluminous publication, of which either the matter or manner would not disgust a young person of taste: the substance of its papers so often consisting in the statement of improbable circumstances, unnatural characters, and topics of conversation, which no longer concern any one living; and their language, too, frequently so coarse as to give no very favourable idea of the age that could endure it.

'Improbable circumstances, unnatural characters'! It is they who inhabit the real world: the City of Invention is peopled by altogether more reasonable folk, with natural and consistent characters. In that City if there is an effect there is a cause; there is relevance, purpose and meaning; it is a wonderful place. She knew it.

I don't think you will have much difficulty in actually *reading Northanger Abbey*, but since you tell me you are now five chapters into your novel – now entitled *The Wife's Revenge* – you may not have a great deal of time at your disposal, so I will give you a quick run-down of the plot.

I do, you see, feel just a little guilty in encouraging you in your literary interest, in the face of your father's disapproval. Only if you manage to pass your exams as well, will I be vindicated; will this family ever be reunited. If you fail, I will get the blame, not you, so don't feel unduly pressurized.

Northanger Abbey, 1798. The novel starts as a literary burlesque and ends as a serious story, in which the heroine – or anti-heroine – has actual, real, recognizable feelings, brought about by social disgrace and public humiliation. Catherine Morland, up to Bath for the season, is asked to stay by her suitor Henry Tilney at his

ancestral home, Northanger Abbey. The Abbey fails to live up to
her expectations of Gothic horror:

> The furniture was in all the profusion and elegance of modern taste.
> The fire-place, where she had expected the ample width and ponderous
> carving of former times, was contracted to a Rumford, with slabs of
> plain though handsome marble, and ornaments over it of the prettiest
> English china. The windows, to which she looked with peculiar
> dependence, from having heard the General talk of his preserving them
> in their Gothic form with reverential care, were yet less what her fancy
> had portrayed. To be sure, the pointed arch was preserved – the form of
> them was Gothic – they might be even casements – but every pane was
> so large, so clear, so light! To an imagination which had hoped for the
> smallest divisions, and the heaviest stone-work, for painted glass, dirt
> and cobwebs, the difference was very distressing.

Henry's father, General Tilney, does arouse her suspicions, however. There is a certain room which no one enters, and the General's
wife died in what could be construed as mysterious circumstances.
Henry, discovering her suspicions – by now quite obsessive – dis-
illusions her with wit, kindness and concern. He's as fine a lover as
any you're likely to find in the Collected Works. They seem on the
verge of marriage. But Catherine is then suddenly and rudely
dismissed by the General, peremptorily sent home by carriage. A
long, uncomfortable and lonely journey.

> What had she done, or what had she omitted to do, to merit such a
> change?
> The only offence against him of which she could accuse herself, had
> been such as was scarcely possible to reach his knowledge. Henry and
> her own heart only were privy to the shocking suspicions which she had
> so idly entertained; and equally safe did she believe her secret with
> each. Designedly, at least, Henry could not have betrayed her. If,
> indeed, by any strange mischance his father should have gained intelli-
> gence of what she had dared to think and look for, of her causeless
> fancies and injurious examinations, she could not wonder at any
> degree of his indignation. If aware of her having viewed him as a
> murderer, she could not wonder at his even turning her from his house.
> But a justification so full of torture to herself, she trusted would not be
> in his power.
> Anxious as were all her conjectures on this point, it was not, how-
> ever, the one on which she dwelt most. There was a thought yet nearer,

a more prevailing, more impetuous concern. How Henry would think, and feel, and look, when he returned on the morrow to Northanger and heard of her being gone.

What's happened is that the General has discovered she isn't an heiress as he had unreasonably concluded – his paranoia (to use a word totally, thank God, unknown at the time. We have too many axe words like this, I believe: cutting through sensibility with a sharp single blow), equalling hers, and in a way serving her right. Henry defies his father and marries Catherine in spite of his disapproval. The novel ends thus:

> To begin perfect happiness at the respective ages of twenty-six and eighteen, is to do pretty well; and professing myself moreover convinced, that the General's unjust interference, so far from being really injurious to their felicity, was perhaps rather conducive to it, by improving their knowledge of each other, and adding strength to their attachment, I leave it to be settled by whomsoever it may concern, whether the tendency of this work be altogether to recommend parental tyranny, or reward filial disobedience.

What do *you* think, Alice, since it does concern you? She is still talking to you, and she knows you are there. You, the reader, are involved in this literary truth, as much as the writer.

When I say to would-be writers, but you must think of your readers, this is what I mean. Not that you must consider markets, and write to fill them, but that, in generosity, forgetting your individual self, you must use your craft to pass on energy and animation and involvement; and if you do it properly, then the craft is understood to be art. You must *aspire*, in order that your readers can do the same.

love from,
Aunt Fay

'An annuity is a serious business'

London, May

My dear Alice,

I am back from a publishing tour of Denmark. Contemporary writers are required, from time to time, to undertake visits to other countries for the purpose of publicizing their work. They will be given an itinerary on arrival and someone from the publishing house delegated to look after them. They will sit in their hotel room and give press interviews at hourly intervals; they will make TV appearances, and radio interviews; they will sign books in bookshops and give lectures at the local university; they will lunch with publishers and book club officials, and breakfast, if they are sensible, alone. There will be no time to think, only to perform. With any luck there will be television in the room (not in Holland, where TV is considered down-market) for late nights, and bath oil and shower caps in the bathroom for early mornings. If there is an hour or two to spare, they will be taken on a sightseeing tour before it is time for their flight. (The word has understandably taken on a double meaning.)

Now an etiquette has grown up around these visits: there is a way to behave and a way not to behave but no one to tell you what it is. There are things to beware, but you must find them out for yourself. To this end, I started a short story which I know I will never finish, it being faultily constructed. £50 if you can tell me why it is unfinishable. (As a clue, I've already told you why *Lesley Castle* never got published.) Herewith:

RETURN TO THE HOTEL ATLANTIC, AARHUS

or

The visiting writer's handbook

Well now listen, sisters! As more and more of us take up our pens and write, so do more and more of us get asked abroad, by publishers, universities, festival organizers and so forth, and we have no rule book to go by, and no handbook to consult, any more in this respect than we do in real life. In real life we have friends to guide us, and magazines to explain ourselves to ourselves, and parents who hold up a mirror (often unflattering) in which we can gaze, but who does the visitor abroad have, in Wellington, New Zealand, or Aarhus, Denmark?

All places of course get nearer home as the cultures of the world become more and more similar, except for the air fare that separates them, and that's a comfort. A woman's group in Madrid is pretty much like a woman's group in Johannesburg. A Women's Studies Department in Oslo is much like one in Melbourne: English is everyone's second language: the divisions in the world are increasingly those of occupation and political opinion, not of nationality. Even so, jaunting abroad, I have nearly jumped from a window of the Lakeside Hotel, Canberra, nearly stepped deliberately in a lorry's path in Stockholm, so great is the overwhelming depression, the sense of isolation that can afflict the visiting writer abroad, in the midst of admiring, even enthusiastic crowds, and all for the lack of a handbook, a little advice, a little forewarning as to what to expect.

Therefore I, Grace D'Albier, aged thirty-five, author of a novel about incest, pass on a little information to you. *Lot and his Daughter* was my first novel, the first one to go into translation, to take the world by storm (publisher's language) and to send me hurtling by Pan-Am around the world, explaining as I go that the novel is not autobiographical; that I made it up. No one believes this, of course. Journalists, in particular, who work so cleverly from the real world, understand description, but not invention. It is not surprising. They lose their jobs if they do invent – novelists get sued if they don't invent. So I, Grace D'Albier, must go round the world, stared at as a victim of paternal and maternal incest: and though my parents still speak to me, they do so in a rather stiff way. They can comprehend that I made it up, but their friends can't.

On the other hand, all over the world women come up to me and thank me, and say my book has helped them; not that the thing, the deed, actually happened to them, but the feeling was always there, and now they need no longer be ashamed that it was. They are part of the new community of the literate; they are released and absolved from guilt, and I have done it.

But there is no comfort at home. My own children look at me askance, especially my oldest son, for Susan in the book had her first child by her father, when she was fifteen, and Susan's mother conceived a child by the son, when the boy was fifteen. Of course I made it up. I am not old enough not to have made it up. But people everywhere believe what they want to believe, not what is true, let alone credible. God knows what the children's friends say. I daren't ask, and they don't say.

Sometimes I think I cannot go on. Here at the Hotel Atlantic, Aarhus, looking out over the cold bright sea and the car-ferry loading bay, and the busy bleak industriousness of normal early morning people, I wonder what I have done to be so separated out from them. And how did it happen that I, who started out as a writer, have turned willy-nilly into a performer? Yesterday afternoon I spoke to five hundred students at the university here: they listened with attention and I felt useful, but a flea – perhaps I picked it up on the plane? – was jumping about inside my new silver Kurt Geiger boots, biting me, and how can you scratch and scream while facing an audience of five hundred? Last night I scratched my feet and ankles while I slept and this morning I find my nails have raked raw weals into my flesh.

But the purpose of this piece is not self-pity, and I know there are few enough people out there in the world to pity me, as I ring for breakfast and it comes with smiles and pleasant looks – black coffee in small Danish cups, rolls and pastries, a boiled egg and their accompanying wafers of cheese, and I have my cake and eat it too.

I pass the time working out details of the Visiting Writer's Handbook. There will be a section for Advance Preparation. Your agent, I will say, under the section ABROAD, will always ask for First Class Air Travel. This will never, of course, be conceded, but serves to make your host nervous enough, if a publisher, to book a rather better hotel for you than originally anticipated (the writer comes out of the P.R. budget); or if a university, or theatre company, to put you up in moderately comfortable, moderately sophisticated households. People who admire your work tend to believe you share their likes and dislikes. Publishers on the whole live well and eat well, and their status and sales are best served if the writer does the same, but academics and feminists believe that if they do not like television, music, meat, soft pillows, central heating, food (even) on moral or practical grounds, then neither will you. I will tell the reader of my handbook of the many strange beds I have slept in abroad – the damp beds of absent grandmothers, the equally damp beds of three year olds; attic rooms and basement rooms: I will refer to the host who said I could have his bath water after him, and before his wife: I will warn the visiting writer that if told, 'We thought you'd rather stay in a private home than in an impersonal hotel' to gently indicate they are mistaken. After a day full of personalities – one's own the most boring of all, I hasten to say – impersonality and peace is most attractive. I have, I will add, for fear of offending the many delightful people whose pleasant hospitality I have enjoyed, broken this rule often and been glad.

I will remark on how tactful and polite the visiting writer presently learns to be. A careless and frivolous remark made in Adelaide one evening, will be repeated in Sydney the next; to whom it most concerns and most hurts. I will advise the writer never, never to speak ill of another writer's works; if forced into a corner, the worst you can say is 'So and so's work is not, I think, counted as great literature'. Never speak ill of the host country, I will say. That is only courtesy. Never speak ill of the host country before last, because that gets back too. Never speak ill, in fact. Hold your tongue and mind your manners.

Be courteous to journalists and considerate of photographers. Remember regional differences. Dutch photographers, for example, will want you to look bleak and grim and as old as possible; lit from above, they will stand you against a stark white wall. Danish photographers love you to laugh and twinkle: American photographers want you to be properly made up and beautiful: Australian photographers want you to look ordinary and like everyone else. Above all, remember this of photographs, those who know you know what you look like, and for those who don't, can it matter? Try and believe it.

Danton D'Albier, the actor whom I married, long ago, the children's father, left me on publication day of *Lot and his Daughter* two years' back. He read the book, against my will, (a kind of rape) and said, 'I never knew you thought like that' and he looked at a photograph of me in *The Times* and said, 'I never knew you looked like that' and I think it was the photograph and not the book that did it. Nevertheless.

... There I stopped. As I say, £50 if you can tell me why I didn't go on. Jane Austen wanted to charge brother Henry 100 guineas for the unfinished *Lesley Castle*, and here am I, actually giving money away.

You write complaining of the dreadful feeling of dry despair which your course in English Literature induces in you: you feel you are suffocating; as if your mouth was being stuffed with dry leaves; as if your brain was slowly dying of some mental poison. It makes you want to scream. How well you put it. I really have hopes for your novel: how is it going? Women in loveless marriages complain of the same feelings: they tremble on the verge of panic; there is something terribly wrong, but they can't quite place it. Or unsupported mothers (well, unsupported except for Uncle State) trudging home up the hill in the rain from Sainsbury's, with a small child on either side: 'Where am I?' they scream, soundlessly, for the wet wind forces protest back into the mouth, 'This is not what I meant at all!' And where are you, Alice, *Persuasion* in one hand and pen in the other, is this what you meant? Are these the joys of literature? – making your mind work where your feelings don't, delving round in your brain for the responses you ought to have, which other people claim to have, and you just don't. It is murder, mental murder, twisting your head to get it into someone else's place (in your terminology) because that person has power over you, to pass you or fail you; accept you in the cultural world or throw you out of it. So you persist, and your mouth chokes up with dry leaves and you write that the character of the second to youngest Bennet sister is undeveloped (you've forgotten her name) because you have been told that is the case: it is universally acknowledged that writers *ought* to develop characters.

Not by me, of course. This kind of criticism, to the writer, is like saying to the mother of her newborn baby, 'But why has your baby got red hair?' implying that surely there was something she should have done about it! 'But that *is* the baby,' she'll say, upset and confused. It is almost as easy to upset and confuse new mothers as it is writers.

Writers are not so rational about the writing of their books, you see, as students of English Literature like to think. They write what they write and if it was different, it would be a different book and have a different title, so fault-finding is self-defeating. And if you think your brain is dying slowly, that your head is held trapped by iron bonds of boredom, it is no more than you deserve. When you study a writer's work in depth you are stealing from that writer: so much he or she offered to you gladly, but you are greedy: you are demanding more.

A writer writes opaquely to keep some readers out, let others in. It is what he or she meant to do. It is not accidental – obscurity of language, inconsistency of thought. The teacher prises open the door so that everyone can rush in. They may well do, but it's not *for* everyone, it was never meant to be.

I think I overstate my case. Only endure! Loveless marriages turn again to loving ones; unwanted children become wanted; the study that bores you today may enlighten you tomorrow. Do not change courses in mid-stream, Alice. Do not abandon Eng. Lit. for Social Studies. Simply write your own book to counteract the danger of too much analysis; synthesize as much as you analyse, and you will yet be saved. So much advice I owe your father. I suppose.

Incidentally, Jane Austen made only £700 during her lifetime, from her writing:

1803: £10 from Crosby, for *Northanger Abbey.*
1811: £140 from the publisher Thomas Egerton, for *Sense and Sensibility.* It came out in 3 volumes, price 15s. £150 from the profits of same.
1812: £110 for *Pride and Prejudice* likewise, published at 18s. The print run was 1,500.
1814: £450 from the publisher John Murray for the copyrights of *Sense and Sensibility* and *Mansfield Park* (since Egerton seemed unable to move them from the booksellers' shelves, produced very small editions and paid very little) and her new novel *Emma.* Egerton excused himself by saying, 'People are more ready to borrow and praise than to buy'.

I make that £860, but it is usual for people to say that 'she made only £700 from her writing during her lifetime'. So that is certainly what you should say in your end of term exams, should the subject come up. Truth is relative in any case, and I read in *New Scientist* that two and two do not·make four, but approximately four, since the very action of adding alters the number, so I daresay £700 *feeling* right, is right.

Love from Fay

P.S. Perhaps someone index-linked the sum and forgot to say? There was shocking inflation between 1800 and 1817. Napoleon and all that.

Let others deal with misery

London, May

My dear Alice,

In *Mansfield Park* there is a young lady, a Miss Crawford, who behaves very badly. She speaks slightingly of the clergy. She is quite without respect for the Admiral uncle in whose household she was brought up, and to whom therefore she should be grateful. She says she has a large acquaintance of various Admirals; she knows too much about their bickerings and jealousies, and of Rears and Vices she has seen all too many. 'Now,' she says, 'do not be suspecting me of a pun, I entreat.' But of course we do. Rears and Vices! Strong stuff! Miss Crawford mocks religious feeling. She remarks, on being shown round the Rushworth Elizabethan chapel, 'Cannot you imagine with what unwilling feelings the former belles of the house of Rushworth did many a time repair to this chapel? The young Miss Eleanors and Miss Bridgets – starched up into seeming piety, but with their heads full of something very different – especially if the poor chaplain were not worth looking at – and, in those days, I fancy parsons were inferior even to what they are now.'

That makes Fanny angry. So angry she can hardly speak. It is the only time in the whole book that she is swayed by unholy passion. She is angry, you see, on Edmund's behalf. Edmund is training to be a parson. Fanny is an unusual Austen heroine: she is good, almost unspeakably good. Edmund is more usual: he is of the Mr Knightley mould. He is kind, noble and instructive. He rather fancies Miss Crawford, in spite of her bad behaviour, perhaps even because of it, and she is certainly the one character in the book with whom one would gladly spend a week on an off-shore island: she is witty, lively, lovely and funny at other people's expense. She is selfish – she unfeelingly makes use of Fanny's horse, to Fanny's detriment, since Fanny seems quite unable to take care of herself – and admits it. Miss Crawford, in fact, doesn't mind being *bad*. Fanny simply can't help being good.

Now Jane Austen started to write *Mansfield Park* in 1812. She had been living in Chawton, with her mother and sister, since 1809. It is tempting to suggest that the struggle between Miss Crawford and Fanny was the struggle going on in the writer between the bad and the good. The bad bit, which could write in a letter to Cassandra, 'Mrs Hall of Sherbourne was brought to bed yesterday of a dead child, some weeks before she expected, owing to a fright. I suppose she happened unawares to look at her husband.' (Now that's far, far worse than anything Miss Crawford ever said.) And the good bit, which struggles to live at peace in a modest home with her mother and sister, and to continue to believe that her father was 'good and kind', (and not, as I tend to believe, the callous and ego-centric model for Mr Bennet), and takes in *Mansfield Park* the personification of Fanny. And even more tempting to go back to Jane Austen's early childhood, and see in that powerful description in *Mansfield Park* of the arrival of a small, timid girl into a strange family – on the whole kindly, but stupid – a portrait of herself, sent away to a school where she nearly died, among strangers, and to suggest that the split between good and bad never, in Jane Austen, quite reconciled and resulting in her early death, started there. The rebellious spirit, raging at being so cast out by mother and father, learning the defences of wit and style – Miss Crawford. The dutiful side, accepting authority, enduring everything with a sweet smile, finding her defence in wisdom – Fanny. So tempting, in fact, that I shan't resist. I shall offer it to you as an explanation of Jane Austen's determination to make the unctuous Fanny a heroine.

And also add that she must have missed her father very much, but in a rather, to us, unexpected way. *Mansfield Park* was the first new novel she wrote after his death – though she worked over *Sense and Sensibility* and *Pride and Prejudice*, novels of which we know he approved. I think she was trying hard, especially hard, to be good: as if without his controlling spirit all morality and self-control might fly away, dissipate, unless everyone was very, very careful. When Sir Thomas, the patriarch, leaves his family to go to Antigua for a time, his fear is – and it seems to Jane Austen a reasonable fear – that if they are without his direction, without his watchful attention, they will behave without restraint and rapidly go to pieces. And so indeed they do – Good heavens! Amateur theatricals!

Mansfield Park throbs with the notion that what women need is the moral care and protection of men. Fanny marries Edmund in the end (of course), 'loving, guiding and protecting her, as he had been doing ever since her being ten years old, her mind in so great a degree formed by his care, and her comfort depending on his kindness, an object to him of such close and peculiar interest, dearer by all his own importance with her than anyone else at Mansfield, that he should learn to prefer soft light eyes [Fanny's] to sparkling dark ones [Miss Crawford's].'

Oh, Miss Austen, what wishful thinking do we not have here! It has come to my notice, Alice, that in the real world the worse women behave, the better they get on. (Discuss, with reference to your female friends, and their mothers.)

Well, perhaps we *should* look to fiction for moral instruction: we should not see it, as we have come to do, as a mirror to be held up to reality. Perhaps writing should not be seen as a profession, but as a sacred charge, and the writer of a bestseller not run gleefully to the bank, but bow his head beneath the weight of so much terrifying responsibility. To be able to influence, for good or bad, the minds of so many! In China they do not have 'novels' in our sense: they have fiction, it is true, but fiction that points the way to good behaviour, both at an individual and a social level. Such works are exhortations to hard work, honour, good cheer, and the power of positive thinking, and sell by the hundred millions. And in Russia any individual writer who flies, in the name of art, or truth, in the face of an accepted group morality, is seen as irresponsible, even to the point of insanity. It is a different way of looking at things. I have some sympathy with it. It is, oddly enough, readers and not writers who believe so passionately that writers should be free to write what they want. I do not think Jane Austen would have thought they should be: certainly not on the evidence of *Mansfield Park*, a book in which virtue is rewarded and bad behaviour punished, and the abominable Julia, disgraced, is obliged to go and live with the awful Mrs Norris. And serve both right.

Your loving Aunt,
Fay

'You have delighted us long enough'

London, June

My dear Alice,

Personally, I see critics as bus drivers. They ferry the visitors round the City of Invention and stop the bus here or there, at whim, and act as guides, and feel that if it were not for them, there would be no City. But of course there would be – people would walk, and save the fares, and make up their own mind where to pause and what to enjoy – but it wouldn't be so convenient, and quite honestly rather tiring, as life can prove to be for the individualist on a packet tour who is glad in the end for a clean mattress in a foreign land, among people who understand.

Quite often people just stay on the bus, and listen to the driver. They can't be bothered getting off, and looking for themselves. They read the reviews, but never the books. I do that, sometimes. Except of course when I'm driving the bus myself, writing the reviews. I tend to stop at every house which comes along, for fear of upsetting the builder. Amazing, I feel, and wonderful that anyone can build a house at all, let alone a good one! Therefore stop and admire – forgo your criticism! Books are not rationed; neither is your enjoyment. The passengers groan, when I drive.

As for the builder, the writer, he listens to what the bus driver is saying, with half an ear, but likes rather more, lurking in the edifice of his own conceit, to hear what the actual visitors have to say. From them, you learn. If everyone hits his head on the lintel in one house, the next time you build, you'll make sure it doesn't happen again. You get tired of saying 'careful' and fetching plaster when people aren't. You build the lintel higher.

A wise writer is not controlled by his readers' response, but is sensitive to it. Jane Austen, certainly, was the latter. In 1814 she collected and transcribed other people's opinions of *Mansfield Park*. By 'other people' read family and friends. She did not bother to quote the newspaper reviews. Perhaps they simply did not matter to her? I select a few collected opinions. Thus:

> Mr James Austen: very much pleased. Enjoyed Mrs Norris particularly, and the scene at Portsmouth.
> Miss Lloyd: preferred it altogether to either of the others. Delighted with Fanny. Hated Mrs Norris.
> My mother: not liked it so well as *Pride and Prejudice*. Thought Fanny insipid. Enjoyed Mrs Norris.
> Miss Burdett: did not like it so well as *Pride and Prejudice*.
> Mr James Tilson: liked it better than *Pride and Prejudice*.
> Miss Augusta Braunstone: owned that she thought *Sense and Sensibility* and *Pride and Prejudice* downright nonsense, but expected to like *Mansfield Park* better and having finished the first volume flattered herself she had got through the worst.
> Admiral Foote: surprised that I had the power of drawing the Portsmouth scenes so well.
> Mrs Pole: 'everything is natural, and the situations and incidents are told in a manner which clearly evinces the writer to belong to the Society whose manners she so ably delineates.'

Everyone, when asked, has something to say, and everyone says something different. There is little consensus. How could there be? My advice to you, Alice, is – if Jane Austen got this response from an already published novel, how much more unhelpful will be the responses of friends and family to your unpublished one? You say your boyfriend has read it and said it is juvenile. What did you think he would say? If your boyfriend wrote a novel about you having an affair with your married professor, would you be inclined to admire it? If he wrote about his passion for your professor's wife, would you enjoy it? You must remember that non-writers do not see fiction as sacrosanct, in the way that writers do. They think it's personal, directly autobiographical and not a gracious suffusing of fantasy, invention, real event and real-er emotion recollected in tranquillity. If you can't stand the heat, keep out of the kitchen: lay down your pen. If you want to publish, send it off to a publisher. Don't hang around waiting for approval. If it's *approval* you want, don't be a writer. There'll always be someone like Mrs Lefroy to say, 'I liked it, but think it a mere novel'.

I think what Jane Austen was looking for was 'permission to invent'. She didn't get it – not since she tried *Lady Susan* and was chided for it. Women were warned – as school children still are – to write about what they *know*, not to imagine. To write about the football field or the school cloakroom, not the polo field or the House of Commons Dining Room. To describe, not to invent.

But novelists don't have to get things *right*. They are under no obligation to describe a real world: they can have the Battle of Waterloo take place in 1820 if they want; so long, that is, as they continue to enable their readers to suspend their disbelief; though in that particular circumstance they would, I can see, be making things difficult for themselves. Writers of fiction can't be *wrong*: they can, I suppose, display so much ignorance, that the reader remembers the writer's existence just at the wrong moment and throws down the book in disgust. Readers like writers to be cleverer than they are. But the strings attaching the real world to the invented world can be knotted and twisted and loosened and tightened and plaited as the writer wishes. He is, you see, in charge.

You will, I do believe, when you have stopped weeping over your boyfriend's cruelty, and when you have read *Mansfield Park*, find the scene when Fanny goes to visit her natural mother at Portsmouth one of the most telling, memorable, real and vivid in the book. It is also the one most likely to be invented. Admiral Foote, if you remember, was surprised she had the power of drawing the Portsmouth scenes so well, assuming she had never been in such a household. And a reviewer of *Northanger Abbey*, in the *Critical Review*, complains that General Tilney seems to have been drawn from imagination – 'for it is not a very probable character, and is not portrayed with our authoress's usual taste and judgement'. To my mind, of course, General Tilney is the most memorable of all the characters in the book, and one of the most probable. More probable, certainly, than his heroic, fault-free son, Henry.

But there you are, you see. Ask one, get one reply: ask another, get another. Get the same reply from everyone, as Jane Austen did, that to invent is bad, to describe is good, and you end up believing the lintel is too low, and not the visitors altogether too long-necked: and next time, you raise it. You do not venture down to Portsmouth again, where you have never been, nor into houses you have never known. You fail to persist, and the visitors never learn to look after themselves, or bend their stubborn necks.

This is most certainly the power of the critics, of the bus drivers. They tell you where it's proper to build and how to build, and not merely what's wrong with the house you've just completed. They know something, but not everything: don't forget it. But listen carefully to the visitors, the readers: listen as you would to a lover. You have the same one-to-one relationship, after all; the same powerful intimacy; the particular connection made through the general emotion. It is like the lamp in the series, glowing fitfully, steadily, or briefly incandescent, depending on how it's placed in relation to the battery and how the current flows. So it's only polite to listen. As to acting on the visitors' suggestions – the same rule holds as acting on a lover's suggestion. You want to oblige, but if you make yourself too much what he wants, or what he says he wants – concepts very often diametrically opposed, alas – you will lose him. You cannot, you see, pretend to be what you are not, without falling into apathy and depression, and becoming boring. The answer, while listening politely to what is being suggested, is very often to do the opposite. To magnify your faults (as seen by the lover, the visitor, the reader) and subdue your virtues. A vulgar aside: 'In real life, as opposed to novels, it's the worst women get the best men.' Discuss.

'The novels of Jane Austen,' wrote an unnamed reviewer in the *British Critic*, 1818, 'display a degree of excellence that has not often been surpassed. . . . This is the forte of our authoress: as soon as ever she leaves the shore of her own experience, and attempts to delineate fancy characters, such as she may perhaps have often heard of, but possibly never seen, she falls at once to the level of mere ordinary novelists. Her merit consists altogether in her remarkable talent for observation.' This critic complains of her want of imagination, and describes it as the principal defect of her writing, but the minute she tries, stamps on her!

Jane Austen stamped on others in her turn. She wrote to her niece, Anna, then engaged on a first novel: 'Do not set your story in Ireland if you have not been there. You will be in danger of making false representations.' When Jane Austen died, Anna threw her MS into the fire, saying it reminded her too painfully of her dead aunt. Any excuse, Alice, any excuse! I shall try not to oblige you similarly.

A great deal of what I have been trying to say to you in the course of these letters was said, rather more gracefully, though in longer sentences, by Walter Scott in 1816.

Walter Scott was a novelist of considerable renown and more than considerable output. He had a family to keep. He wrote thus in the *Quarterly Review*, in 1816, on the subject of Jane Austen's *Emma*. I abridge considerably. Men of letters then clearly had time at their disposal. But try not to skip. He writes beautifully:

> There are some vices in civilised society so common that they are hardly acknowledged as stains upon the moral character, the propensity to which is nevertheless carefully concealed, even by those who most frequently give way to them; since no man of pleasure would willingly assume the gross epithet of a debauchee or a drunkard. One would almost think that novel-reading fell under this class of frailties, since among the crowds who read little else, it is not common to find an individual of hardihood sufficient to avow his taste for these frivolous studies. A novel, therefore, is frequently 'bread eaten in secret'; and it is not upon Lydia Languish's toilet alone that Tom Jones and Peregrine Pickle are to be found ambushed behind works of a more grave and instructive character. And hence it has happened, that in no branch of composition, not even in poetry itself, have so many writers, and of such varied talents, exerted their powers. It may perhaps be added, that although the composition of these works admits of being exalted and decorated by the higher exertions of genius; yet such is the universal charm of narrative, that the worst novel ever written will find some gentle reader content to yawn over it, rather than to open the page of the historian, moralist or poet. . . .
>
> The judicious reader will see at once that we have been pleading our own cause while stating the universal practice, and preparing him for a display of more general acquaintance with this fascinating department of literature, than at first sight may seem consistent with the graver studies to which we are compelled by duty: but in truth, when we consider how many hours of languor and anxiety, of deserted age and solitary celibacy, of pain even and poverty, are beguiled by the perusal of these light volumes, we cannot justly condemn the source from which is drawn the alleviation of such a portion of human misery, or consider the regulation of this department as beneath the sober consideration of the critic.

You will see, Alice (if you have not skipped), that Mr Scott regards novel reading as diversionary tactics against the regimen of reality. *Littérature engagée*, the socially useful novel, was yet to appear. Read on. I have trimmed and cut for your benefit.

... The author of novels was, in former times, expected to tread pretty much in the limits between the concentric circles of probability and possibility; and as he was not permitted to transgress the latter, his narrative, to make amends, almost always went beyond the bounds of the former. Now, although it may be urged that the vicissitudes of human life have occasionally led an individual through as many scenes of singular fortune as are represented in the most extravagant of these fictions, still the causes and personages acting on these changes have varied with the progress of the adventurer's fortune, and do not present that combined plot (the object of every skilful novelist), in which all the more interesting individuals of the *dramatis personae* have their appropriate share in the action and in bringing about the catastrophe. Here, even more than in its various and violent changes of fortune, rests the improbability of the novel.

In other words, in real life we can have effects without causes, causes without effects. Not so in fiction.

... A style of novel has arisen, within the last fifteen or twenty years, differing from the former in the points upon which the interest hinges; neither alarming our credulity nor amusing our imagination by wild variety of incident, or by those pictures of romantic affection and sensibility, which were formerly as certain attributes of fictitious characters as they are of rare occurrence among those who actually live and die. The substitute for these excitements, which had lost much of their poignancy by the repeated and injudicious use of them, was the art of copying from nature as she really exists in the common walks of life, and presenting to the reader, instead of the splendid scenes of an imaginary world, a correct and striking representation of that which is daily taking place around him.

In adventuring upon this task, the author makes obvious sacrifices, and encounters peculiar difficulty. He who paints from *le beau idéal*, if his scenes and sentiments are striking and interesting, is in a great measure exempted from the difficult task of reconciling them with the ordinary probabilities of life: but he who paints a scene of common occurrence, places his composition within that extensive range of criticism which general experience offers to every reader.

In other words, Alice, the new novelist (i.e. Jane Austen) risks more, because her readers know more. But these two lines of mine are a very crude representation of what Walter Scott had to say. I speak hurriedly, for a hurried world: you don't have much time: your telephone will go and everything will suddenly change: Scott's readers had time to finish sentences, however long, and patience to fillet out niceties of meaning which I do not even attempt to convey. To continue:

... We, therefore, bestow no mean compliment upon the author of *Emma*, when we say that, keeping close to common incidents, and to such characters as occupy the ordinary walks of life, she had produced sketches of such spirit and originality, that we never miss that excitation which depends upon a narrative of uncommon events, arising from the consideration of minds, manners and sentiments, greatly above our own.

You see, they were all obsessed by it. The novel must be used to set before the reader examples of good behaviour. I am frequently asked why I write about anti-heroines and anti-heroes, and not role models, and all I can say in my defence is that what I write is what I write and there is not much I can do about it.

... Upon the whole, the turn of this author's novels bears that same relation to that of the sentimental and romantic cast, that cornfields and cottages and meadows bear to the highly adorned grounds of a show mansion, or the rugged sublimities of a mountain landscape. It is neither so captivating as the one, nor so grand as the other, but it affords to those who frequent it a pleasure nearly allied with the experience of their own social habits; and what is of some importance, the youthful wanderer may return from his promenade to the ordinary business of life, without any chance of having his head turned by the recollection of the scene through which he has been wandering.

One word, however, we must say on behalf of that once powerful divinity, Cupid, king of gods and men, who in these times of revolution, has been assailed, even in his own kingdom of romance, by the authors who were formerly his devoted priests. We are quite aware that there are few instances of first attachment being brought to a happy conclusion, and that it seldom can be so in a state of society so highly advanced as to render early marriages among the better class, acts, generally speaking, of imprudence.

But the youth of this realm need not at present be taught the doctrine of selfishness. It is by no means their error to give up the world or the good things of the world all for love; and before the authors of moral fiction couple Cupid indivisibly with calculating prudence, we would have them reflect, that they may sometimes lend their aid to substitute more mean, more sordid, and more selfish motives of conduct, for the romantic feelings which their predecessors perhaps fanned into too powerful a flame.

Who is it, that in his youth has felt a virtuous attachment, however romantic or however unfortunate, but can trace back to its influence much that his character may possess of what is honourable, dignified, and disinterested? If he recollects hours wasted in unavailing hope, or saddened by doubt and disappointment; he may also dwell on many which have been snatched from folly or libertinism, and dedicated to studies which might render him worthy of the object of his affection, or pave the way perhaps to that distinction necessary to raise him to an equality with her.

In other words, better to pine, better to suffer the pangs of unrequited love, than to be flippant, frivolous and drunk. Remember that, Alice!

Even the habitual indulgence of feelings totally unconnected with ourself and our own immediate interest, softens, graces, and amends the human mind; and after the pain of disappointment is past, those who survive (and by good fortune those are the greater number) are neither less wise nor less worthy members of society for having felt, for a time, the influence of a passion which has been well qualified as the 'tenderest, noblest and best'.

Oh, Alice, has your relationship with your professor, however unfortunate, not given to your character much of what it now possesses that is honourable, dignified and disinterested? Has not your recent indulgence of feeling softened, graced and amended your mind? I hope so. And if only, had you not wasted hours in unavailing hope, had you rather dedicated the time to studies which would render you worthy of his affection, raised you to an equality with him – how different things might have been! Or, again, might not.

Or, as your father would say, 'for God's sake, Alice, stop mooning around and get on with your work.'

I know Fanny Price is a masochistic idiot, standing round there in the Park letting others walk all over her. I agree with Mrs Austen that she's insipid – but she got her man in the end! Perhaps you should practise a meek, self-righteous virtue, and see where that gets you. That is, of course, if you still *want* your man. It is always amazing, to those not concerned, to observe the stern passions which quite ordinary young men arouse in the hearts of young women.

With much love,
Fay

P.S. You do not win your £50 bet, which makes a change. 'Return to the Hotel Atlantic' was an agreeable title, little more. It had no shape, no inbuilt tensions. I had no real idea what was going to happen next, or worse, what was the point of the story. Not only did I have no peg to put the coat on, I had no coat. Grace D'Albier was rather a nice idea; but incest is not a rather nice idea. What were they both doing in the same story? Having said that, the fact that they were might well have been the point, and had I ended with silver boots full of blood, we might have been getting somewhere. But I doubt it: it was all too uneasy a grafting of fiction onto fact to work. It veered out of invention into description and back again: they never fused. You don't win your £50. *You* just said you found it boring. You and your twin Miss Augusta Braunstone, as aforesaid. Nothing changes.

A gently lingering illness

London, June

My dear Alice,

I shall write a little about the manner of Jane Austen's death. I want to get it over. I find it upsetting. I suppose as pleasure spills over through the centuries, so grief does too. She is presumed to have died from what is now called Addison's disease – an insufficiency of the adrenal glands. The adrenal cortex fails to work properly for one reason or another – it can be T.B., or a fungal infection, or a tumour, or by virtue of the body turning against itself, deciding that what is benign is harmful and setting out to destroy it and succeeding – that is, as a consequence of the autoimmune process. The condition these days affects one in every hundred thousand people. (John F. Kennedy is rumoured to have had Addison's disease – it is nowadays contained by synthetic steroids: and it was liberal doses of cortisone, they say, which gave him a jowly look and sent him racing down the White House corridors after totally inappropriate secretaries. But as I say, they'll say anything.)

In Jane Austen's day there was no cure, and indeed the disease was not even identified, let alone named, until the 1840s. Dr Addison – who else? – then discovered it, in the proper sense of the word. To Jane Austen, her friends and doctors, it must have been a completely mysterious event: a gently creeping illness, of an undefined nature, particular to her and her alone, which might end in death, but might not. Their hope, as time went on, must have failed.

The early symptoms of the disease are langour, lack of appetite, exhaustion, irritability, and a disinclination to physical or mental effort. (I, for one, find alterations in the mental state, as a symptom of illness, more distressing than mere physical disability, or even pain. Is the personality, really, no more than the sum of the body? I find it hard to accept.) The skin looks dirty, the mouth blotches. 'The body wastes,' wrote Addison, 'the pulse becomes smaller and weaker, and the patient at length gradually sinks and expires.' And so she did.

In our terms death comes by hypoglycemia, shock and cardiac arrest. If only we could have their language and our drugs.

That is enough. The dying should be accorded some privacy.

I think she probably just gave up. I find it hard to believe that when death occurs by the auto-immune system, by the body turning against itself, that the unconscious will is not involved. As with cancer, when normally harmless cells proliferate and by so doing cause their agreeable host such damage. Death, in Addison's disease, comes eventually as a result of upset – 'the inability to withstand severe or even minor stresses without going into shock'.

Enough, enough! Surely, that's enough . . . .

When Jane Austen was so ill, they say, she rested in the living room on an arrangement of three chairs. Her mother kept the sofa. Enough!

I think writers can kill themselves off early enough, as they can the extensions, the different versions of themselves that go into their books. They flesh them into existence, and wipe them out again. In the end, I am sure, they could altogether fictionalize the original body, from which the shadows spring to take up their habitation in the City of Invention. One could leave this world easily enough and take up one's existence over there, in That Other Place.

I tell you this to comfort you. It isn't pleasant to think of her dying of a lingering illness which modern medicine would diagnose and cure. But death is only a part of life; one cannot see it, when recently bereaved; one sees only pain, waste, anger and humiliation, the worst and not the best. Only with time does the end sink back into proportion, become part of the whole and not the definition of the whole. And that's another reason why the death of children is so particularly dreadful, and early deaths worse than later ones – there is less lived time available into which dying time can be swallowed up and incorporated. Alice, we will, as they say, be a long time dead. You must carve your living self as sharply into the Rock of Eternity as you can. Please send your novel off; don't do as you threaten and forget it. Of course it's more than likely to be rejected and come back, and of course you will then feel rejected and discovered in your presumption. But if you embark on these things, you can't draw back. Or you'll be just a snail-trail on the Rock . . .

No? Well, I stick by it. You did it, I warned you not to, now take the consequences. You made your bed, as your mother's mother would say to my sister and me, now you must lie upon it. I remember making her extremely angry by replying, 'I don't see why. One can always lie on someone else's'.

How did your exams go? Did you know I am to have tea at a tea parlour in Covent Garden with your mother and father? I worry rather about this. I feel the chairs will be made for narrow modern hips and the sandwiches will be tough, bran-enforced rolls filled with ground sesame, and the tea will be herbal and the sugar brown, and your father somehow not be in his proper ambience. But you never know.

With best wishes,
Aunt Fay

London, July

My dear Alice,

I am extremely sorry about your exams. Is it my fault? I suppose so. Your mother has cancelled tea at Covent Garden.

Why don't you try an American university? I'll pay.

Much love,
Aunt Fay

A publisher's offer

London, July

My dear Alice,

This is wonderful, astonishing and gratifying news. Publishers mean what they say. If they say they will publish a novel, that is what they mean to do. If they say they are delighted by *The Wife's Revenge* that means they think they will make a profit out of it. (If they say 'impressed', they mean the critics will like it, if not necessarily the public.) If they say they will pay you £700 for it, consult an agent, and one who is not an outrunner for the Publishers' Association but one who sees his duty to his client clearly: that is, to fight publishers. I will send you names. But do remember that more money now means less later. You only start getting royalties when the advance has been paid back. If you have any faith in your book – go for greater royalties and a smaller advance. On the other hand, of course, the greater the advance, the greater the P.R. budget is likely to be . . . .

Publishers grade books into what they judge to be 1. good/good books; 2. bad/good books; 3. good/bad books; and 4. bad/bad books. Categories 2 and 4 they reject; 2 with many apologies and explanations, 4 with mere rejection slips. Their judgment, of course, may be wrong. From their response I imagine they are placing you in 3, where most of the bestsellers dwell. Since they have accepted your book, I should not worry too much about their view of it. At least they're not suggesting you change the setting from a university to a Fish Factory, on the grounds of a revival in plebeian settings.

What do your parents say? Aren't you excited? I am! Will you settle down to 'be a writer' or will you go to UCLA as planned? It would save me money if you did the former, but I very much hope you won't. I am sure I have written to you, in earlier letters, about the dangers of being a writer. Why not go to UCLA *and* write? It is possible to do both: you have proved it is possible to do what so many of your colleagues claim is impossible: to study English

Literature *and* write: to analyse with one part of your brain; synthesize with the other. Perhaps the hot sun and the blue sea will stop you writing: I still argue in favour of postponement while wishing you a world bestseller.

Mind you, you never read *Persuasion*, did you! Tricky days.

You are probably wise to join the new celibacy movement, in the company of your professor's wife. I am glad you two got together. It was on the cards. Leave your professor to his new junior lecturer, and your boyfriend to your professor's sister, and read *Persuasion*.

Let me give you the first paragraph:

Sir Walter Elliot, of Kellynch Hall, in Somersetshire, was a man who, for his own amusement, never took up any book but the Baronetage; there he found occupation for an idle hour, and consolation in a distressed one; there his faculties were roused into admiration and respect, by contemplating the limited remnant of the earliest patents; there any unwelcome sensations, arising from domestic affairs, changed naturally into pity and contempt, as he turned over the almost endless creations of the last century – and there, if every other leaf were powerless, he could read his own history with an interest which never failed – this was the page at which the favourite volume always opened. . . .

The rest is up to you.

With love,
Aunt Fay

The marvel of creation

London, August

My dear Alice,

It is time I started another novel – there is one waiting in the far recesses of my mind, like an octopus beneath a coral reef, occasionally putting out a feeler or two, prodding quite painfully into my conscious mind. I will have to respond, I can see: dive down and haul it out, and up into shallower, brighter waters, where I can get a good look at it, and then catch it and kill it and chop it up and fry it in batter and serve it up in some Quick Food Café. The book you mean to write is never the book you do write. A piece of fried octopus on the end of a fork, compared to the mysterious hidden majesty of the living thing. Never mind.

No? Too ridiculous a metaphor? You may be grateful that I mean to stop diverting myself by writing letters to you and get on with *Amygdala*. The word means the part of the brain where rage is centred. The novel is set two hundred years in the future. Publishers and agents warn me against it – not in so many words, of course, but with a faint look of pained bafflement in the face. They are good at that.

I shall send you a reading list. I hope you don't think this is patronizing of me. You have sold more copies of *The Wife's Revenge* in three months than I have of all my novels put together (well, in this country at least. Let me not go too far). I am glad to be wrong about so much; I still maintain that it is better to read than not to read, and I still deplore what you refer to as your 'general amiable illiteracy'. Can you be developing some kind of house style?

Sometimes, I think, the exhilaration of all this being so great – of ideas, notions, fantasies, speculations, claims false and valid, advice good or bad, the pattern made by altering truth as day melts into day, is great enough to make us immortal. These things have been, and so in a sense always will be: they are not finite in time. Only our bodies are that. Let them blow us all up if they want, reduce the planet to ashes (as they say) – the leap between nothing and something, once made, is always made. It is the marvel at creation that can't be destroyed: not the creation itself. *Emma's* pages here in the real world, may in the end yellow and curl and go unread. Emma's voice may falter and fade into a final silence: 'But, Miss Bates, we have a difficulty here . . .' And yet, I do believe, though all else falls, the City of Invention will stand.

It doesn't matter, Alice, little Alice. Here and now. Think here and now. Your mother tells me you have your own hair back again. (What you call greasy mouse, and she calls healthy, clean and natural.) Is that progress, or a talisman against success, a surfeit of attention? I hope you bear them both well. And I have been asked to tea *at your house* by your mother, and your father has consented to be there too, so long as I don't talk about novels, writing, feminism, or allied subjects. I shall try to keep the conversation to pets and food, and be very happy.

With all my love, your Aunt
Fay

An alternative reading list
for the easily distracted

Any bestseller of any decade. Bestsellers are not generally – or indeed often – works of literature, but will give you a background against which to place more serious works. They appealed, at the time, to a common sensibility.

You should have a general nodding acquaintance with the following writers – no matter that they make strange bedfellows:

FROM AMERICA: Edith Wharton, e.e. cummings (*The Enormous Room*), Sinclair Lewis, Nathanael West, Budd Schulberg, John Updike, Philip K. Dick, Joseph Heller, Philip Roth.

FROM ENGLAND: Edmund Gosse, Robert Tressell, Flora Thompson, P. G. Wodehouse, Aldous Huxley, Robert Graves, Evelyn Waugh, Rosamond Lehmann, Graham Greene, Salman Rushdie.

FROM ELSEWHERE: Chekhov (the short stories), Turgenev, Boris Pasternak, Jean-Paul Satre, André Malraux, Georges Simenon, Herman Hesse, Gunter Grass, Gabriel Garcia Marquez.

I expect you to get on with about fifty per cent of these. Add them to the more opaque writers you find on your college reading lists and you should be able to engage anyone in a literary discussion at any dinner table in the land, and not to show off your knowledge but simply because you take pleasure in books, and know at least a few main routes in the City of Invention.